THE
SHIFT

17 INSPIRATIONAL STORIES TO REFLECT GOD'S DIVINE EXPANSION WHEN YOU "SHIFT" TO HIM

FOREWORD BY DR. KISHMA A. GEORGE

COMPILED BY AMBER K. ABNEY

The SHIFT @ November 2025
Compiled By Amber K. Abney

Published in the United States of America by
ChosenButterflyPublishing LLC

www.ChosenButterflyPublishing.com

ISBN: 978-1-945377-94-5
First Edition Printing
Printed in the United States of America
November 2025

CONTENTS

FOREWORD

Dr. Kishma George

There comes a moment in every life a crossroads, a breaking point, a divine intersection where a choice must be made: to stay where you are, or to shift into what God has destined you to become. The Shift: 17 Stories of Divine Transformation is a sacred and timely collection of such moments.

When Elder Amber K. Abney, a true visionary shared this project with me, I immediately sensed the weight of Heaven resting upon it. This is not just a book of stories, it is a movement of testimonies. Each narrative within these pages is a living altar, a place where pain met purpose, where brokenness collided with healing, and where surrender unlocked transformation.

Each story in this collection is a prophetic blueprint a reminder that when you surrender fully to God, He doesn't just repair your life He *transforms* it. These are voices of overcomers, carriers of glory, and vessels who encountered the weight of pain, only to rise with the oil of purpose. Their testimonies speak with power, purity, and fire.

As you turn these pages, I challenge you to reflect not only on the stories told, but on the story you are living. What is God inviting you to shift from? Where is He calling you to shift to? Transformation is not a distant dream, it is a divine promise, waiting on your yes.

May *The Shift* serve as your divine invitation to move with boldness, with faith, and with expectation into the fullness of who God has called you to be.

Blessings,

Dr. Kishma George

www.kishmageorge.com

A CHILDHOOD OF STRUGGLES AND SURVIVAL

K. Renee Smith

K. Renee Smith is a Human Resources professional with extensive experience in employee relations, labor management, and HR policy across military and civilian sectors. She holds dual master's degrees in Human Resources Management and Leadership, a bachelor's in Human Ecology, and is pursuing a doctorate in Strategic Leadership. Recognized for her excellence with multiple awards, Renee is also a proud mother of four who enjoys meditation, reading, serving her community, and attending church.

Highly dedicated to serving people, Renee has built a reputation for fairness, integrity, and problem-solving throughout her career. Her commitment to excellence extends beyond her professional accomplishments to her faith and community service, where she actively seeks to uplift others and create a positive impact in every area of her life.

Dedication To Alexis, James Jr., Myles, and Kelley-Rose, This piece is written for you not to burden you with the pain of my past, but to give you understanding, context, and a window into the journey that shaped me. I write these words so you may see the strength that comes from surviving, the courage it takes to heal, and the power of breaking cycles of pain and generational strongholds. I write for you so that you may know your history, but also see that your future is not defined by it. May these pages remind you that even in the midst of hardship, resilience, love, and hope can flourish. My story is yours to learn from, to draw strength from, and to carry forward as a legacy of truth, courage, and healing long after I am gone. Wanda, how could I possibly forget you? You've played such an instrumental role in shaping who I am today—thank you from the bottom of my heart.

Early Memories in Pensacola

One of my earliest memories takes me back to the early 1980s in Pensacola, Florida. The city buzzed with life, day and night—fried food smells in the air, music echoing from juke joints, and heat that clung to everything. Yet, for me, the palm trees and sunlit beaches didn't define my childhood. My world was far smaller, more unstable, and much darker.

At the time, I lived with my mother, Trish. Everyone else called her Pat, but she preferred we call her "Trish" instead of "Mom." She had three children, each with a different father, and a history of struggles that I didn't understand at the time. As a child, I simply longed for her love, yet I couldn't find it. Only years later did I come to understand the complexities of her life—her cognitive challenges, past trauma, and cycles of unhealthy relationships.

I was the middle child, too young to protect myself but old enough to remember the pain. My older sister, Tan, was about twelve then—far too young to be the caretaker she often became. My youngest sister, Ruby, was just a toddler, unaware of the chaos surrounding us. At the time, I was only four, still holding on to the belief that safety was something to be taken for granted, though I was beginning to understand otherwise.

The Night That Shattered Innocence

One night in particular stands out, marking a turning point in my young life. My mother went out with her boyfriend and we were left at his mother's house. Initially, it seemed like just another night, but I woke up with a heavy, sinking feeling in my chest. Something was wrong, though I couldn't quite name it. I crawled to Tan, whispering, "Someone's bothering me." Tan, still a child herself, tried to comfort me, but there was nothing she could do.

I woke up several times that night, each time more disoriented than before. By the fourth time, I was in a nightmare I couldn't process. There was blood where I lay. The next thing I remember is waking up in a hospital, my body bruised and broken in ways a four-year-old should never experience.

Following this occurrence, home as I had known it no longer existed. The Department of Health and Rehabilitative Services

(HRS) took control of our lives. Tan was placed in a group home, while Ruby and I were placed in the care of our aunt and uncle. My life, as I had known it, was forever altered.

Hunger and Neglect

Before our placement in foster care, neglect was a constant in Trish's life. Survival often meant finding whatever scraps we could and hunger was a constant companion. One Valentine's Day at school, I received a bag of treats from my teachers, a small gesture of kindness that felt like treasure. But when one of my mother's boyfriends saw it, he threw it away. That was a blow, but it wasn't the end. Tan urged me to find the discarded food and I crawled into the dumpster to retrieve what I could—leftovers, candy, anything that could ease our hunger.

We lived in a tiny duplex under a bridge, surrounded by the noise of the nearby juke joint. The apartment was hardly a home. Water didn't flow and I often had to climb onto the refrigerator to open one of my mother's beer cans—still unaware of alcohol but desperate for something wet. The only light in that darkness came from our elderly neighbor, who, despite her own limited means, offered us food and care. But one day, she was gone—taken away in a body bag. Her kindness, too, vanished from our lives.

Unsafe Refuges

Despite the neglect and violence we faced, we were never removed from Trish's custody until I was hurt. When Trish struck Tan with a skillet, knocking her eye out of its socket, we remained. When school reports went unheeded, we stayed. Only my injury forced the system to step in.

At my aunt and uncle's house, we hoped for a refuge, but it was far from safe. Their frequent fights and tension made the house uneasy. My aunt's unpredictable moods made it hard to feel secure and I soon became the victim of inappropriate contact. It was a stark reminder that danger can lurk anywhere—even where protection is expected.

The Anchor of Church

The strain at my aunt and uncle's house eventually led us to foster care. Though I felt relief at first, uncertainty lingered. Sometimes Trish showed up, but more often, she didn't. Through it all, one force began to shape our lives: church.

Our foster mother, Mrs. Christine, introduced Ruby and me to church. It became our anchor, a place of prayers, songs, and stories of a loving God. Here, I encountered Mr. Jimmy, a preacher who became a lifeline. I will never forget the day he stood in court, Bible in hand, and told the judge, "They will not be separated." Ruby and I were kept together, a rare blessing in a world determined to split us apart.

Living with Mrs. Christine was both growth and struggle. I made mistakes, acted out, and often found trouble. Yet her steady presence taught me discipline and responsibility. After three years, Ruby and I were adopted, though the transition brought new challenges.

Adoption and New Struggles

Moving to Milton, Florida, and being adopted into a new family brought its own struggles. I resented my adoptive parents at first, especially my adoptive mother, who seemed threatened by the closeness Ruby and I had with our father. The family grew when my adoptive mother brought in five more children, increasing tension. The trauma of my earlier years lingered and new challenges surfaced.

As I grew older, the household dynamics shifted in ways that left me feeling unsafe and unheard. In time, concerns arose that led to outside involvement and once again I was placed back into foster care. Being separated from Ruby during this time was devastating and I was left to navigate a system that too often failed to protect the very children it was meant to serve.

Becoming a Mother

Amid this turmoil, I had my daughter Alexis at the age of eighteen. She became my saving grace; the person I vowed to protect no matter what. For her, I would do anything to ensure she never faced the same pain and fear I had endured.

Serving While Raising a Family

Joining the United States Army was not a calling only a necessity— it was how I would provide for my child and create a different path forward. Service gave me structure, purpose, and the ability to care for Alexis. Yet research shows that children who endure deep trauma often gravitate toward unhealthy relationships later in life. Sadly, I did not escape this truth. My choices in partners were not always the best and I found myself in a marriage that mirrored patterns of my past.

Out of my marriage, however, came three more blessings: James Jr., Myles, and Kelley-Rose. My children ground me, even in the hardest times. Through them, I found reasons to keep striving, keep growing, and keep praying. I can only hope that I did not parent them vicariously from the shadows of my childhood but instead offered them the love, stability, and guidance I once longed for.

Transformation and Advocacy

Reflecting on those years, I see that despite the abuse, neglect, and hunger, there was always a thread of hope—through neighbors, church, and Mr. Jimmy's intervention. I learned that survival isn't just enduring—it's finding grace, protection, and resilience. Even in the darkest moments, I felt God's hand guiding me, shaping me for something greater.

Today, I give back as a Court-Appointed Special Advocate (CASA). I ensure that each child's voice is heard in court and that their well-being is at the center of every decision. This work is deeply personal—a way to honor my journey and be the advocate I once needed. It reminds me daily that healing is possible, that purpose can be born from pain, and that no child should face battles alone.

Epilogue: Defined by Strength

My story is not one defined by fear, abuse, or neglect. It is defined by strength, compassion, faith, and transformation. From the courtroom to the church pew, from the hospital bed to the foster homes, and now into advocacy, every chapter has contributed to the woman I've become. As I stand for others, I do so with the unshakable belief that hope—when nurtured—can break even the most painful cycles.

THEN, EVERYTHING CHANGED

Michele Peterson

I was born in Altus, Oklahoma, into a military family on an Air Force base. My early childhood was spent in North Dakota, where I was raised until the age of twelve, when my family split apart, moved to the South and, at fifteen, I was kicked out and left to navigate life on my own. What followed were years of survival and hard lessons—I found myself dealing drugs, stripping, and hustling just to make it through. Yet even in the chaos, resilience was being forged in me.

At thirty, I chose a different path. I earned my GED, pursued higher education, and eventually graduated from Georgia State University with a bachelor's degree in accounting. Today, I use my journey to lead and teach others the path to debt freedom, showing that financial empowerment is possible for anyone willing to do the work. Beyond finance, I am deeply passionate about guiding the next generation. Through my girls' empowerment initiative, I create safe, uplifting spaces where young women can grow in confidence, resilience, and purpose. My story is proof that no matter where you begin, it is possible to rewrite your life with strength, determination, and faith. Faith is what kept me and God is who held me.

My life once seemed like a picture of perfection. We were a typical Air Force family—my parents, my two sisters, a live-in grandmother, and me—living on base. I hold on to glimpses of those happy moments: camping trips, fishing with my dad, and Christmases overflowing with gifts. Then, everything changed.

I was twelve when the first domino fell. One Sunday, after church, at a smorgasbord, I overheard my mom and older sister giggling about a man. My mom revealed he was my sister's father, a fact she'd previously hidden by simply calling him her boyfriend. In that moment, I learned two things that would shatter my world: my eldest sister had a different father, and three days later, my mother abandoned me and my other sister—just a week before Thanksgiving. It took me many years to understand my mother's actions, but I eventually recognized that she suffered from a severe, undiagnosed case of narcissism. She was incapable of providing genuine support or empathy. Our relationship has always been this way; we hardly speak, and at times, years pass by without contact. Her abandonment, both physical and emotional, was a symptom of her deep self-centeredness. In her world, everything revolved around her, including our lives and our pain.

Our lives were upended. My father, an angry and abusive alcoholic with PTSD from his time in Vietnam, struggled to provide any stability. The instability and violence escalated, and just before Christmas break, I was torn from the home I knew. My father had molested my older sister, leading to our separation and further trauma. We were placed in two different foster homes. I can vaguely remember walking into that home a week before Christmas; a Christmas teddy bear with the year embroidered on it was all I got that year, while surrounded by strangers. I suppose this is when the desire for security became a strong craving in my relationships.

A Downward Spiral

At twelve, my life did a 180-degree turn. The night before I was to be reunited with my mom and sister, I was molested by my uncle while lying in bed with my grandmother and him. Angry and defiant, I rebelled. I fell into a life of fighting, promiscuity, street life, drugs, theft, exotic dancing, and hustling. By age fifteen, my behavior got me thrown out of my mom's house. I was listed as a runaway, picked up by the authorities, and then escaped a runaway home with another teenage girl. We made our way to the projects in Pensacola, Florida, where we went on a spree of breaking and entering and theft. My friend was arrested, and while I was evading the police, a man in an empty apartment cornered me. He sexually assaulted me at knifepoint, forcing me to masturbate after I lied and told him I had an STD. He had a limp leg, and I thought I could push him and escape by jumping out the window, but he grabbed me, and my attempt failed.

I left Pensacola and headed back to Fort Walton Beach, Florida. From there, I began a hitchhiking journey to Louisiana with two other girls. It was an adventure that took us two days and several good Samaritans to reach our destination. Louisiana, however, became the worst experience of my life as I was raped twice. The first attack was by a gang leader, and the second was by a friend of my then-blood boyfriend. The last assault almost cost me my life. As my attacker robbed me, he told me he would have to kill me because of my boyfriend. He choked me, leaving a thumbprint and two fingerprints on my neck that people would later mistake for hickeys. The authorities contacted my mother and her response was typical of her narcissistic nature. She told them to send me back to Florida, saying I shouldn't have been in Louisiana anyway. There was no concern for my well-being, only frustration at my inconvenience. The rape kit performed was not only humiliating, it was painful. Once I returned, I continued the street life, living on the edge. Shelter was easier to come by as I rented a two-bedroom apartment "under the bridge" and my older sister lived with me. She became the caregiver, cooking and cleaning while I dealt crack and paid the bills.

At seventeen, I was stabbed six times in a fight, coming within half an inch of death. My mother came to visit me in the hospital and I remember the hope that swelled in my chest. Maybe now she would finally see my pain and offer comfort. But she left without me, the hope quickly turning to ash. It was a profound act of emotional abandonment. The next day, I went back to the streets and started dealing drugs just to survive. Shortly after, ten girls jumped me, one biting me in my face, and I knew I had to get out of there. I decided to move to Orlando to avoid ending up dead or in jail.

The Hustle and the Shift

In Orlando, at seventeen, I started stripping on Orange Blossom Trail at a topless bar. I began frequenting nightclubs, winning numerous dance contests. I was recruited by some exotic dancers who did male and female revues and started performing in a nightclub owned by a retired NBA player, a spot where Orlando Magic players often hung out. It was there I met a dancer named Smoove. We began a relationship and I moved with him to Atlanta, Georgia. Shortly after arriving in Atlanta and sleeping on friends' floors, Smoove and I rented our own apartment and lived together for a year.

At eighteen, I walked into the Playboy Palace to apply for a job, only to realize it was a fully nude strip club. I wasn't comfortable with intentional nudity, but I needed the job and I was already in the industry. For much of my life as a young lady, I carried an "I don't care" attitude that served as a shield against the pain of my past. It was a default setting I used to survive. We eventually broke away and started our own company, XXXposure Entertainment, traveling to perform at various nightclubs in the southeastern region. We had five female and four male dancers. I danced for a total of three years and then retired. I actually hated the idea of it.

At twenty-two, I began a seven-year same-sex relationship. My choice to be with a woman was heavily influenced by the disgust and unreliability I had experienced with men, but it was also a subconscious search for a secure, maternal bond I never had. I loved the sense of sisterhood and always having someone around. It became very toxic, though, as she was unstable, jealous, and bipolar. The decision to shift stemmed from a very violent breakup with her. It was during this time that I was convicted and knew God was not pleased with the way my life was going. I began seeking God and attending church and I realized He had His hand over my life all along. I should have been dead many times over.

A few months after leaving that relationship, I met my ex-husband. It seemed to be a perfect match and a security blanket for my crazy life, a promise of a new, stable beginning. While in this relationship, at age thirty, I decided to go back to school. I had to get my GED, but the taste of education, and the doors it could open, propelled me forward. I went on to achieve my bachelor's degree in accounting from an accredited university, Georgia State University. After graduating, I made a pivotal choice. My deep desire to be a mother was not being fulfilled and I made the conscious decision to sacrifice my career for a role as a nanny for two doctors. The children became my very own and I poured all my love into raising them until they were ten and eleven. It was during this time that I was well-compensated and formulated a plan to become completely debt-free in my fifties. I also attended a Dave Ramsey event where I learned the essential tools for financial freedom. I was so inspired by my own journey—from a bad credit score in the 500s to the 800s—that I began teaching financial literacy classes to my fellow members of the congregation. The character I gained from being a nanny and loving those children transformed my "I don't care" attitude into one of empathy and responsibility. I finally started caring about people and building genuine relationships.

For the entirety of my relationship with my ex-husband, a critical void existed: a deep, unfulfilled need for quality time. I begged for it, but it was a plea he never answered. He consistently chose to hang out with everyone on the street, giving them more time than he ever gave me. This neglect and emotional distance were a major factor that contributed to our eventual divorce. I married at thirty-seven, but the marriage was complicated. The first year was challenging as I had an ectopic pregnancy and surgery soon after our wedding day. My husband had some health challenges, and over time, it shifted our marriage and we should have sought counseling.

At fifty, I had gained the clarity and strength to leave and embrace my freedom. It took reaching thirty years of age for me to truly recognize that God had a purpose for my life all along, protecting me through every single trial. This truth was brought into sharper focus by my emotionally devastating divorce. Amidst the painful unraveling of my marriage, a friend introduced me to Atlas Training, an emotional intelligence leadership program. What was meant to be a distraction became the foundation for my healing. Through Atlas, I gained the tools to navigate the divorce with grace and strength, even as my ex-husband hired a private investigator, had me tracked, stalked me, and almost drove me to my breaking point. Atlas not only gave me the resilience to endure this ordeal but also helped me process and heal from all the childhood trauma I had endured.

I learned that my voice matters, that I am enough, and that my story is not just a tale of survival but a testament to my leadership. My character was not forged by defiance but by my faith and the unwavering belief that God was carrying me. I am exactly where I am meant to be at every given moment because He said so. My pain had a purpose and it became my mission to create a safe space for others. My ultimate goal is to launch a teenage empowerment initiative, offering a haven for young girls so they don't have to endure the trauma I did.

Today, in my fifties, I am living a life that was once just a dream. I manifested being completely out of debt, having my house paid for, and traveling the world. The freedom to choose and the freedom to go give me a peace that is unexplainable. This sense of fulfillment extends to my work; I am in service as an alumni and student leader with Atlas, helping new students find their own path to healing. I have always been one to look on the brighter side, even in the midst of the most difficult times, and my life is now a testament to that unwavering optimism. The very things that once broke me are now being used to build up the next generation. This is my "shift."

THE RESILIENT ONE: A JOURNEY FROM BROKENNESS TO BREAKTHROUGH

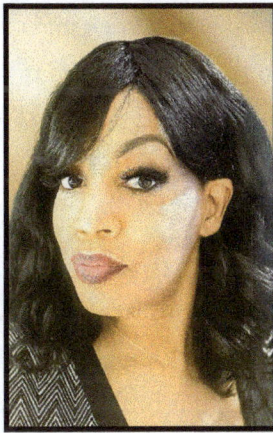

"Hey there! I'm Cameka, a 45-year-old powerhouse from Atlanta, Georgia. My journey has been anything but ordinary. I grew up in and out of foster care and I was adopted at just eight months old. Life threw some serious curveballs my way and I faced serious hardships early on. I spent an eternity looking for love, and myself, and made very dangerous and life-changing decisions throughout. But God... God knew I was destined for more even when I didn't. I wanted to turn my life around for me and my kids and didn't know how or where to start.

If there is one word that captures who I am today, it's **RESILIENT!**

I've lived through storms most people wouldn't believe. Born into chaos, in and out of foster care, and adopted at just eight months old, my earliest experiences were filled with uncertainty, instability, and pain. I spent years searching for love, identity, and a sense of belonging, which led me down some dark and dangerous roads. I made choices that changed the course of my life and not always for the better.

There were moments when I didn't think I'd survive. Moments I didn't want to. I carried shame, regret, and questions that haunted me for years. I tried to fix everything on my own (for myself, my kids, and extended family), but I didn't know how. I felt lost, broken, and invisible.

But God...

Even when I didn't believe in myself, He did. Even when I thought my story was over, He was writing a new beginning. He saw value in me when I saw nothing but broken pieces.

This book is the beginning of me telling that story. *Resilient: A Journey from Brokenness to Breakthrough* is more than just a memoir. This is my testimony of my life! It's a raw, honest, and unfiltered look at the battles I've fought, the mistakes I've made, and the grace that pulled me through. It's about true transformation and it's not the kind that happens overnight but the kind you fight for, cry through, pray over, and grow into.

If you've ever felt like you've gone too far, fallen too hard, or messed up too much to turn it around, I want you to know I've been there too. And I'm here to tell you: **you can come back from anything.**

My prayer is that my life story gives hope to someone who feels stuck in theirs. Because if God can heal me, restore me, and still use me, then He can do the same for you.

Now my story is being shared in a book, and I hope it sparks inspiration and hope in others who've faced similar battles. Life's been a wild ride and I'm here to show that there's always a way forward!

THE JOURNEY OF THE PRODIGAL DAUGHTER

Toforaya Rodriguez

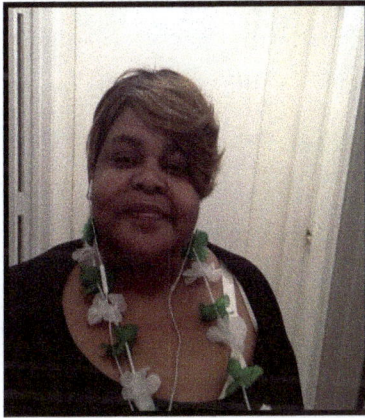

Bio:

I was born Toforaya Lynn Jordan in the summer of 1969 in Newnan, Georgia. I was the oldest of three children born to my mother and the second oldest to my father. In 1971, my mother relocated the family to Atlanta, Georgia. I attended East Point Elementary, Cleveland Avenue Elementary, Crawford Long Middle School, and later, as a sophomore, I enrolled at Walter F. George High School. But I didn't finish. I abandoned school, lost in the confusion and pain I was experiencing during that time in my life. At a very young age, I was forced to grow up faster than any child ever should. This is not just a story. This is my life. And it is also a warning to any young girl and her family.

Dedication

In loving memory of my mother, Arlena S. Matthews. Your strength, love, and unwavering faith remain my guiding light.

Acknowledgments

First, I thank my Heavenly Father for carrying me through this journey and for never letting me go, even when I wandered far away. To the love of my life, my husband, Benjamin Franklin Smith, Jr., your support and steadfast love have been my anchor. To the panel of the Shift, my family, and my friends, your prayers and encouragement have been a covering I could never repay. To Smalley and Deborah Turman, my spiritual parents, I thank you for speaking life over me and reminding me that God still heals and restores.

Finally, I would like to extend my heartfelt thanks to Ms. Amber K. Abney and Dr. Caarne White for giving me the opportunity to share my story and for supporting me throughout this journey. Your support means more than words can express. I am forever grateful.

Introduction

Luke 15:11–32 tells us the story of a prodigal son. But what happens when the prodigal is a daughter? This is not just a retelling of a parable—it is my life. I was born on July 15, 1969, the oldest child of a single mother. From a young age, I carried responsibilities too heavy for a little girl. At 15, I married, believing I was grown enough to begin a new life. What I found instead was abuse, pain, and loss deeper than anything I had experienced at home. Like the prodigal son, I wandered far—not just from family but from myself. Each wrong turn, each wound, each betrayal seemed to push me further into darkness. But grace never left me. The Father was waiting all along. This book is a peeling back of layers—not to shame but to set free. It is the story of "Baby," a girl who endured unthinkable trauma at the hands of her own father. It is also the story of redemption, healing, and the Father's unwavering love that calls us daughters again.

The Story

"No Daddy, Don't."

From the beginning, Baby carried a weight too heavy for her small shoulders. As the oldest child of a single mother, she grew up quickly. While other little girls played with dolls and dreamed of birthday parties, she learned how to cook, clean, and care for her younger siblings. Responsibility made her appear strong, but deep down she was still just a child who longed for someone to protect her. In her heart, "Daddy" was supposed to be that protector. To a little girl, a father is like Superman—the one who swoops in when danger comes, the one who wipes tears and promises safety. Baby believed in that picture. She wanted it to be true. But instead, her father became the very one she needed saving from.

It happened at night, when the house had grown quiet. Baby was already in bed when she felt something strange in the air as if a shadow had crept into her room. She opened her eyes to see the faint light from the hallway spilling across the floor. For a moment, she thought it might be her sister. But standing there was her father, dressed in khaki shorts, moving silently into the room. Her heart dropped. She remembered locking the door. *How did he get in? Why is he here?* Confused and afraid, she whispered, "Daddy, what do you want?"

He crossed the room slowly, promising things no child should ever hear. His voice was calm, almost casual, but his presence felt heavy, wrong, and terrifying. Baby lay still, frozen between fear and disbelief, praying silently that this was just a bad dream. But it wasn't. Her father climbed onto the bed, speaking sweet words twisted into something evil, and then he took from her what was never his to take. She wanted to scream, but the fear was louder. She wanted to run, but her body wouldn't move. When it was over, he slipped away without a word, leaving Baby motionless in her bed, her innocence gone.

Shaking, she got up and ran to the bathroom. She turned on the shower, scrubbing her skin as if water could wash away what had just happened. But no matter how hard she tried, it wouldn't come off. Some stains are too deep for soap and water. Only God can cleanse them. That night, she curled up on the sofa, wide awake, wondering if anyone would ever understand the horror she had just lived through. Tears rolled down her face as she whispered prayers: "God, please see me. Please don't leave me here. Please help me."

But the nightmare wasn't over. Her father returned again, pressing in with the same darkness. This time, Baby prayed with everything in her: *God, stop this. God, I'm scared. I don't know how to get out.* And then silence. A holy stillness filled the room. Her father fell asleep before he could harm her again. That was her chance. With courage that could only have come from above, Baby slipped out of bed, tiptoed to the door, and made her escape. She ran into the night, trembling but determined, believing that if he came after her, someone outside would hear her crying. God had opened the way. She made it to a friend's house, where she was finally able to call her sister. Her sister came quickly, gathering Baby into her arms and taking her somewhere safe. That night marked the beginning of her deliverance. God had heard her cry.

The Silence and the Shame

But rescue didn't erase the pain. When Baby finally found the courage to speak her truth, many in her family refused to believe her. Instead of comfort, she received threats. Instead of support, she heard cruel words meant to silence her. People whispered behind her back, accusing her of things no child could be guilty of. The shame was unbearable. She felt as though she had been wounded twice—first by her father's hands and then by her family's disbelief. Baby wrestled with feelings of worthlessness, isolation, and despair. She wondered if she would ever be free from the chains of her past.

Running at Fifteen

By the time she turned fifteen, Baby thought she had found her way out. If life at home meant pain, maybe marriage could mean freedom. She believed she was grown enough to take control of her life. But stepping into adulthood too soon only opened the door to more hurt. The abuse continued in new forms—emotional, verbal, and physical. Baby discovered that pain doesn't vanish just because you change addresses. Wounds carried inside the heart will follow wherever you go.

God Intervenes

And yet, through every dark valley, God's presence remained. Even when she felt forgotten, He was near. Even when she had no words to pray, her tears became prayers that reached His throne. Slowly, God began to show her that her story wasn't over. He had plans for her life—plans of freedom, healing, and hope. In moments of despair, she picked up her pen and wrote her pain onto paper. In seasons of loneliness, she prayed. And though healing didn't come overnight, little by little she began to sense God piecing her back together.

The Long Road to Healing

Healing requires more than forgetting. It meant facing the truth of what happened and choosing to surrender it to God. Baby learned that forgiveness was not excusing the wrong—it was releasing the hold it had on her. She chose to forgive her father, not because he deserved it but because she refused to stay bound by his sin. She began to speak life over herself: "I am not a victim. I am a survivor. I am not forgotten. I am God's beloved daughter." With each declaration, chains broke. With each step, light replaced darkness.

The Redemption

Now Baby stands as a testimony to God's restoring power. Her earthly father failed her in the worst way, but her Heavenly Father never abandoned her. He met her in her lowest moment and lifted her out of despair. Today, she walks free—not because the past has been erased but because the Father has rewritten her future. Baby has discovered that even the most broken story can become beautiful in the hands of God. This is the journey of the prodigal daughter—not just wandering away from home but wandering away from herself, only to be found, healed, and loved by a Father who never let's go.

Message to Survivors

To every survivor, I declare: You are not a victim—you are a survivor. Your trauma does not define you, Christ does. Healing is possible. Freedom is yours. All is well with your soul. To the perpetrator: God's mercy is available even to you. Repent, seek Him, and you will find forgiveness. To the onlooker: You don't know the depths of another person's pain, so silence is better than careless words.

Conclusion: Returning Home

The prodigal daughter's journey is not just about running away—it's about coming home. Baby's story reminds us that no matter how deep the pit, God's arm is deeper. No matter how strong the chains, God's love is stronger. Today, I stand free. Not because the past didn't happen but because God stepped into my past and rewrote my future. This is the Father's love—it meets us at our lowest and calls us daughter again.

I Became Living Proof

Clintnesha Castleberry

Bio:

Clintnesha Castleberry is a proud United States Army veteran and devoted mother of twin daughters. With over 20 years of experience in customer service and human resources, she has built a career rooted in dedication, professionalism, and a commitment to helping others. A passionate sports fan and avid traveler, Clintnesha enjoys exploring new places and experiences. Her true calling has always been working behind the scenes, where she finds fulfillment in supporting others and making a positive impact wherever she can.

Wife. Soldier. Mom of three. Daughter. Aunt. Sister. Niece. Granddaughter. Cousin. Friend. She was all of these and more.

Her name was Clintnesha Matheny. She also went by Nee, Nesha, or NeeNee.

It was a special time of the year where her five-year-old son Rayvon graduated preschool and her six-year-old son Vincent graduated kindergarten. She also had a precious and beautiful two-year-old daughter, Natalia, who was a mama's gal.

Nesha's mother-in-law (RIH), Mary D. Baldwin, flew down from Jersey City, NJ a few days ahead to participate in her only grandchildren's graduation ceremonies. She baked personalized treats and took them to the school on the special day. It was always such a joyous occasion spending time with Mary.

The graduations were so nice. All of the school personnel and students enjoyed the personalized treats. As the week was coming to an end, it also meant that it was time for Nesha's mother-in-law and the kids' grandmother to return back home to NJ. Nesha did all she could to try to talk Mary into staying a while longer with her and the kids. Her main concern was driving on the road on a major holiday. Nesha had made a vow never to drive on the roads during major holidays.

Well, Mary decided to still return home to NJ. Nesha did not have to drive 97 miles to Atlanta International Airport because there was a company called Groome Transportation Shuttle that charged a small fee to transport passengers to and from Columbus, GA, to the airport and Mary agreed to go on it.

On May 25, 2012, Nesha left home with her three children and mother-in-law to head to the Groome company. The children and Nesha said their goodbyes and gave lots of hugs and kisses. There were even a few tears shed by Nesha and Mary. Nesha did not return home right away. Instead, she took the kids to the mall and let them pick out a book and bought them a cookie. She sat in the mall a couple of hours longer to allow the kids to play while she talked on the phone.

After some time passed, Nesha and the kids proceeded home, which was about 20 minutes from the mall. It was a bright and sunny day at about three o'clock in the afternoon. Nesha was about six minutes from home on a road she had driven for the past six years when a very unexpected automobile collision happened.

Nesha's car was stalled in the road. The kids were screaming. Nesha started looking around pretty shaken up and distorted. She realized she was in a great amount of pain and that she and the kids were bruised and scratched up pretty badly. The front windshield was cracked into thousands of pieces that looked as if they would all crumble and fall if just one gust of wind blew. People had stopped to try to help.

Nesha's automobile was stuck in the drive position, which kept the doors locked. People were pulling the doors and yelling that the car looked as if it was going to catch fire. Nesha was not all the way conscious to make out what the people were yelling outside her automobile. Someone called the police and lots of emergency personnel arrived on the scene.

After some time, they were able to pry the driver's door open, get the car put in the park position to unlock the other doors, and rescue the children. Someone assisted Nesha with getting out of her seat belt and the vehicle. Nesha yelled, "I cannot walk." The individual saw that her ankle was twisted and stuck under the gas pedal. After helping to carefully remove her very deformed ankle, they carried her to the ambulance, who then put a neck brace on her and Vincent and transported them to the nearest hospital.

Shortly after Nesha's arrival to the hospital, a police officer came in to ask her for her driver's license and she handed it to him, still in shock, disbelief, tears, pain, and everything else imaginable. It was later told to Nesha that she called her Aunt Angela, yelling and screaming in tears to please pray for her and her children as they had been in a horrible automobile accident.

It was also later told to Nesha that one of the people who were helping at the scene took her phone and called the last name in the call history, which was her mother-in-law who was just about to board the plane and head home to NJ. Mary couldn't believe what she had just heard. She ran out of the airport and flagged down a Groome van to bring her back to Columbus ASAP and to the hospital.

What Nesha didn't know at the time was that her other two children were in a critical condition and had been airlifted to a hospital in Atlanta, GA. There, Natalia and Rayvon lay almost lifeless on life support. Mary called the Army command to send a Red Cross message for her son and Nesha's husband, Vincent, to be sent home right away.

Vincent was granted emergency leave to fly home from Korea on an almost 15-hour flight. The message he received was somehow not clear and he was told that his wife and children were deceased. My

God, to be on a 15-hour flight home thinking your whole family is gone. That's a lot.

The news spread like wildfire to the entire family and friends of Nesha and Vincent. Nesha's dad Clinton took a leave of absence from work and came down from SC. Her mom, Dorothy Jean, made a call to her sister-friend Amber to meet the airplane in Atlanta to be with her youngest two children in her place until she could get there. Nesha's auntie Angela also took a leave of absence from work to go and be by her niece's side. What in the world was happening all so fast and suddenly?

Nesha was transported to the Atlanta hospital by a basketball teammate from high school, Candy, and was in a wheelchair due to needing surgery on her deformed ankle.

Her husband Vincent arrived and was very disturbed and angry. Nesha and family lived in the Ronald McDonald House for the next three weeks, praying, crying, silence, hugs, visitors, and going from one room to the other room to look at both children lying on life support. Nesha had to speak to 12 doctors a day, six for each child. The time came for her to only talk to God about what to do next.

Nesha's husband left her side after only one night in the Ronald McDonald House and only two days at the hospital. He decided to go back to their home in Columbus, GA and remain there. Nesha had expected him to be by her side. He was not. She knew this was not good. This was adding to her pain.

Nesha was thinking about her six-year-old son Vincent who was going to have to live without a brother and sister now. What? Why? How?

Nesha had to unexpectedly put her surgery off for another month to plan a funeral for her youngest two children, Rayvon (five years old) and Natalia (two years old). Nesha was lost, confused, hurt, sad, and a mix of thousands of other feelings and emotions.

Her other closest sister-friend, ZaBrina, came to her side immediately to assist her from start to finish. ZaBrina left her own dad during Father's Day and went to be by Nesha and her family's side. The children were taken off of life support and a short time after were pronounced deceased on June 17, 2012.

What in the world? How in the world? Why in the world? What just happened? What is happening? How did this happen? Why did something so bad happen to a good person, a great mom, and a beautiful family?

Nesha had more people visit her home in two weeks than the entire six years she lived in it. The funeral was planned in her hometown of Pensacola, FL. A mother who had to paint her daughter's nails, pick out a casket, and attend her children's funeral. A mother whose six-year-old son crumbled and cried almost every day struggling to understand. A mother who had to hide her emotions and tears to comfort and pray with her son. A wife whose husband distanced himself from that day forward until this later led to their divorce after 15 years of marriage.

After Nesha returned to Columbus, she was told that she was charged with the accident. She had to turn herself into the authorities. With tears running down her face, she did and immediately bonded out. What was happening? A soldier who was never in trouble in her life, who never had surgery, who never wore a hat or rode in a cab until she joined the military, had just had her entire life flipped upside down in less than a month.

Nesha had her surgery, which led to her not being able to drive for nine months. She depended on friends and family to help her and her son Vincent. These misdemeanor charges carried a black cloud over her for many years of her life. It affected any job application due to the way this showed up on background checks. She felt like she continuously had to relive the accident because of this.

Nesha also had to have a second surgery on her ankle, which led to her having arthritis and tendinitis. She walked in this pain practically every day, which was a constant reminder of her tragic loss.

The SHIFT of a new hope, a new strength, and a mom of one child. Nesha realized God was the only one she could talk to no matter the hour. She told herself that if she never believed in Heaven or Hell before, then she definitely did now because where were her children? Would she truly ever see them again in Heaven?

"Faith is the substance of things hoped for and the evidence of things unseen." – Hebrews 11:1

For the next six years or so, Nesha built her life and the life of her son in more isolation and full of tears and faith. She leaned on little Vincent for strength and comfort like no other. She did not believe she could call family and friends because she thought they would get tired of hearing her vent, cry, and yell. She thought no one would understand because no one could relate to such a sudden and unexpected tragedy. Prayer and therapy became her medicine.

Nesha blamed herself, thinking she had done something terribly bad and this was her punishment from God, except she could never think of what was so bad for her to receive this type of punishment.

Veteran. Daughter. Aunt. Sister. Niece. Granddaughter. Cousin. Friend. Great-Aunt. She is all of these and more.

"For I know the plans I have for you," declares the Lord, *"plans to prosper you and not to harm you, plans to give you hope and a future."* – Jeremiah 29:11

I have to keep going. God spared my life for a reason and a purpose. I am loved. I am blessed. I am His. I AM.

"I can do all things through Christ who strengthens me." – Philippians 4:13

I Became Living Proof.

Becoming Anchored: Faith, Family, and the Journey Within

Kavanah Brooks

Childhood: Love, Lessons, and Silent Battles

I was born into a middle-income African American home where love was always present even though life was not always easy. My parents worked hard to provide for us and they created an environment where we understood that family was the foundation we could always return to.

My mother was the heart of our home. She was kind, giving, and deeply rooted in her faith, but she also carried her own private battles. From the time I was born, she fought illness. I grew up watching her smile through pain, cook dinner when she was exhausted, and put her children's needs before her own. Her illness was a constant presence in our lives, but she never allowed it to define her. Instead, she used it as a reminder that strength is not found in how easy life is but in how faithfully we live through it.

I remember one day as a young girl, helping in the kitchen, my mother was instructing me on what to do. She wasn't feeling well—her face showed her pain, her hands trembled slightly—but her voice was steady as she spoke to me. She told me, "No matter what happens in life, always carry yourself as a woman of virtue. Do not let the world tell you who you are—let God show you who you are." Those words settled deep in my spirit and they have guided me ever since.

My parents had three children together, but our family was larger than that. My father had eight children in total. Some of them came through his marital affairs and one was welcomed purely out of love after an outside relationship. To the world, this might have looked messy. But to us, it was simply family. My mother never turned away a child. She raised us all with dignity, teaching us that the circumstances of our birth did not determine the worth of our lives.

Growing up in a home where love and dysfunction lived side by side taught me how to balance the good and the bad. I saw my parents deal with the impact of drugs on people around us and I saw the wounds that infidelity left behind. Yet, I also saw forgiveness. I saw resilience. I saw a love that was not perfect but that refused to let hardship win.

Even as a child, God was showing me that life would not be without storms. But He was also showing me that storms reveal strength.

Reflection: Even in a home filled with challenges, love and support became the foundation of who I am today.

Scripture: *"Train up a child in the way he should go; even when he is old he will not depart from it."* – Proverbs 22:6

Takeaway: The values instilled in us during childhood remain guiding lights throughout our lives.

Motherhood: A New Beginning at Twenty

At twenty years old, my life changed forever. I became a mother.

Holding my son for the first time, I felt a rush of emotions I could not explain. I was young, scared, and unsure of what the future would hold, but I also felt a love so deep it brought me to tears. The weight of responsibility hit me immediately: this little life depended on me.

Being a single mother was not the plan I imagined for myself. There were nights when I sat on the edge of my bed, exhausted and overwhelmed, wondering if I was strong enough for the task. I worried if I could provide enough, guide enough, and love enough. But every time I called on God, He reminded me that He equips the ones He calls.

I leaned heavily on my support system. Family members stepped in to help when I needed rest or when I was working to provide for us. My "village" became an extension of God's grace in my life. They reminded me that I was not alone, even when it felt like the world was on my shoulders.

Raising my son was not without challenges. There were days of tears, tight finances, and loneliness. Yet there were also days of laughter, joy, and victory. One memory that stands out is when he was in elementary school and came home with a small project he was proud of. He looked up at me with eyes that said, *"I am Donta the Great, Mom?"* and I realized in that moment that he wasn't just looking for approval—he was standing on the wings of God, for His reassurance, safety, and love would cover him through life. And I promised him that day that I would always make sure he knew it.

Years later, my son grew into a strong young man. He carried the lessons of resilience I tried to teach him and he went on to become a successful businessman and dad. Watching him achieve his goals filled me with pride and gratitude. My little boy who once looked to me for stability had now built stability for himself. And I knew that every sacrifice, every tear, and every prayer had been worth it.

Reflection: Becoming a mother at a young age shaped my resilience and showed me the strength hidden within me. **Scripture:** *"Her children rise up and call her blessed."* – Proverbs 31:28 **Takeaway:** Motherhood is not about perfection but about love, sacrifice, and growth alongside our children.

Loss & Faith: Learning to Lean on God

The most difficult seasons of my life have come with loss.

In 2001, I lost my mother. Her illness had been a part of my life for as long as I could remember, but nothing could prepare me for the moment she was gone. When she took her final breath, it felt as if a part of me had been taken too. For years, she had been the anchor, the teacher, the quiet strength in our family. Now I had to step into the role she left behind.

Then, in 2020, I lost my father to COVID-19. His passing was unexpected, sudden, and heartbreaking. The pandemic already carried so much fear and when it touched my family in this way, it was devastating. Yet even in that pain, God had given me a gift.

Before both of my parents passed, I had dreams that revealed their time was coming. I did not fully understand it at the time, but I see now that those dreams were God's way of preparing me. They were not warnings meant to frighten me—they were blessings meant to strengthen me.

Still, grief is heavy. After my father's death, I often asked, "Who will I lean on now?" The loneliness felt unbearable. But slowly, I began to realize that the answer had been with me all along. I would lean on God.

Reflection: Losing both parents tested the depths of my soul, but it was in that brokenness that I discovered the unwavering presence of God. **Scripture:** *"The Lord is close to the brokenhearted and saves those who are crushed in spirit."* – Psalm 34:18

Takeaway: Grief may feel like the end, but faith reveals it as the beginning of deeper strength and understanding.

Divorce & Identity: Walking Through the Fire

Divorce was another shift I never expected.

It is one thing to lose someone to death. It is another to lose them to brokenness. My divorce wounded me deeply. It brought shame, questions, and the painful feeling of failure.

There were days when I relived the same loneliness I felt after losing my parents. Days when I wondered if I would ever feel whole again. But in those moments, I wrestled with myself. Just like the man in the Bible who wrestled until morning, I wrestled with my fears, my anger, my anxiety, and my grief. And like him, I came out changed.

Divorce forced me to find my identity again—not as someone's wife, not as someone's daughter, but as God's child.

Reflection: My divorce wounded me, but it also taught me to call on my faith and lean on God's healing hand.

Scripture: *"My grace is sufficient for you, for my power is made perfect in weakness."* – 2 Corinthians 12:9

Takeaway: Every ending is also a new beginning when we place our lives in God's hands.

Strength & Growth: Embracing My SHIFT

Now, at fifty years old, I look back over my life and see the hand of God in every chapter. My SHIFT—my journey through childhood, motherhood, loss, divorce, and growth—has been filled with both pain and beauty.

I understand now what the old Negro spiritual means when it says, "I'll understand it better by and by." For years, I struggled to make sense of the hardships I faced. But today, I see that each one shaped me. Each one refined me. Each one strengthened me.

I have learned to love others where they are, not where I wish they would be. I have learned the power of boundaries and the importance of peace. I have learned to recognize the signs of stress—even something as simple as a chair filling up with clothes—and to pause, breathe, and invite healing.

God has been my steady anchor. He doesn't always give me what I want, nor what I feel I deserve—but He always gives me what I need.

Reflection: My journey has not been easy, but it has been necessary. Through every trial, I have been shaped, refined, and strengthened.

Scripture: *"They that wait upon the Lord shall renew their strength; they shall mount up with wings as eagles."* – Isaiah 40:31

Takeaway: Growth comes when we reflect, release, and redefine. Strength is born when we choose to rise again each day.

Closing Encouragement

If my story encourages you in any way, let it be this: you are not alone. Whatever you are facing—whether grief, parenting, loss, or heartbreak—God is with you.

Allow yourself to reflect on your journey. Release what no longer serves you. Redefine who you are in Christ. And press forward.

"So do not throw away your confidence; it will be richly rewarded. You need to persevere so that when you have done the will of God, you will receive what He has promised." – Hebrews 10:35–36

This is the truth I stand on: God has brought me through and He will do the same for you.

My SHIFT is still unfolding. And so is yours.

Broken but on the Road to Forgiveness

Elder Carla R. Hunter

Bio:

Elder Carla R. Hunter, a native of Baton Rouge, Louisiana, currently resides in Stone Mountain, Georgia. She is a lay counselor, teacher of God's Word, and a psalmist.

Carla began her singing career at the age of eight in the children's choir at True Love Baptist Church in Baton Rouge, Louisiana. Her professional singing career began in 1996 with James Bignon and the Deliverance Singers. Carla has also worked with the internationally known Pastor Hope David and the Fusion Choir, singing backup, and also with Wura Grant and the Emmanuel Cantata under the leadership of Pastor David Grant.

In March of 2012, Elder Hunter accepted the call to preach the gospel and the uncompromised Word. She delivered her first sermon on March 18, 2012 and was ordained a year later by Bishop Gary Hawkins, Sr. Elder Hunter received her biblical training through VOF Faith Institute and Impact University.

God continues to open doors of opportunities for Elder Hunter by allowing her to serve on a board as a director for a non-profit organization called Glorious Helping Hand that helps battered and displaced women. She is also the founder of Virtuous Girl, LLC, a ministry and apparel business for women of all ages. She has a heart for women and her motto is: "I'm equipped, empowered, authorized, and qualified to help you change your life."

Elder Hunter is also the founder and host of a Facebook Live series called *"Sassy for the Savior."* You can see it every second and fourth Wednesday at 8:00 p.m. EST under the name Carla Hunter. She is also a graduate of Southern University, where she holds a marketing degree. She is the proud parent of two children, a son and a daughter.

I thought I was living a great life. Married, college educated, great career, living in a suburb of Atlanta. We purchased a new home, built it from the ground. I had two kids, my son and daughter. My life was how I imagined it. My marriage was not perfect, but I was in it for the long haul.

One Friday at work, my now ex-husband called me and insisted that we go for dinner. I thought to myself that was strange because he never called me during work hours. As I sat in my car for lunch, the Holy Spirit told me that he was going to ask me for a divorce that night. My stomach sank. I finished my lunch and went back to work.

I got home from work and started to get dressed for our outing and he came upstairs to tell me that he forgot to get a sitter for the kids, so we could not go out that night. We ordered some food instead. After eating dinner, I retired for the evening. As I was lying down, my ex entered the room and proceeded to tell me that he was not happy with our marriage. "Let's separate and work on the marriage," he said and this would give him the opportunity to date other people. I said no to this request. What was the purpose of doing that?

So, I started seeing changes in his behavior. His phone started ringing late at night and on family outings, he started driving by himself. I remember my daughter had a dance recital; he didn't ride with us. This man told me that he had people to see and places to go after the recital. I was shocked and I just looked at him in disbelief. My kids even asked me why he wasn't riding with us. I didn't have an answer for them, so when he returned home, I told him to tell the kids why he didn't ride with us and why he didn't go to dinner with us. He just looked at me, clueless, lost for words. This behavior continued for months.

My ex-husband and I owned a jewelry and accessories business and we hosted parties at people's homes. When we hosted these parties, we worked together as a team. We never went alone. One Sunday, after church, he told me he had scheduled a party. I told him to let me get dressed so we could leave. He told me I didn't need to go because he had partnered with some ladies who were selling lingerie. I asked what that had to do with us because we always worked the party as a team, so what was different this time.

He pleaded his case and went by himself. Prior to him leaving for the event, we received a phone call from his sister. She called to inform us about his mother. His mother was in the hospital, her health was failing, and it was not looking good. So I told him he needed to go home to see about his mother. My ex-husband told me that he would do this party and from there he would get on the road to go see about his mother.

I asked him what time the party was scheduled to end. He said around 9:00 p.m. I told him he needed to come home because that was too late to be getting on the road to travel. When we had to travel late at night, I was the one who drove. So he said he would drive until he was tired then he would get a hotel room. I said to him, "Okay, just let me know what city you stop in to sleep."

So he called and told me he was stopping in some town in Tennessee. The next morning, I got up and called my niece and told her to call me and let me know what time he arrived to town because I didn't believe he was telling me the truth. What my ex didn't realize was that I knew the drive, time-wise, because I had driven it many times. So based on the city that he told me he stopped in and the time, I knew he had made it to Kentucky. Something did not add up. This man had lied to me. He never left Atlanta after a party.

He got up that Monday and drove from Atlanta to Kentucky. I was so upset, but I didn't say one word to him.

He continued on with his mess. One Saturday, I had to go to work. While at work my girlfriend called me and I shared with her what I was going through. I began telling her what my ex was doing and I gave her the details about this trip. That's when I put it all together and realized that he was cheating.

I called him from work and asked him to show me the receipt from where he stayed in Tennessee. He told me that he paid with cash and no receipt was given. I told him to stop playing with my intelligence. The hotel always gives a receipt. I told him that if he couldn't show a receipt, he needed to get out of my house. So he left. This was the shift in my life.

After my ex-husband left, I was left to raise two kids by myself. This separation broke me down mentally. I can remember that my mind was so consumed with the breakup that I would forget to cook for the kids. They would tell me they were hungry. I spent many days in bed crying.

I thank God that I had a good supervisor at work who had compassion for me. Some days I would go to work and the tears would start. I couldn't get them to stop. My supervisor would have my coworker take me outside to get myself together or she would send me to see a therapist. My life was in shambles, so I had to make a decision: was I going to let the breakup destroy me or was I going to get up and fight? I chose to fight.

I had a conversation with God. I let Him know that the breakup took away my confidence, I was depressed, and I didn't know how to get back on track. I made God my best friend. I began working on myself.

The first thing I did was read *The Purpose Driven Life* by Rick Warren. This book was the first part of the puzzle that put me back together. Secondly, I started getting up every morning, spending quality time with God. I would give Him seven minutes in the morning. In these seven minutes, I would read my devotional and scripture, worship, and pray to set my day. In my prayer time with God, I asked Him to heal me but also to make me whole again.

The third thing I had to do was to forgive my ex-husband and his mistress for the infidelity. I spent months praying, asking God to help me forgive the two of them. I did this because I didn't want them to have a hold on my life. I didn't want to be that person who became bitter. Forgiveness is a process. Sometimes we think just because we say we forgive, it's done. That is far from the truth.

I understood that forgiveness for me had nothing to do with the other parties involved. Matthew 6:14–15 tells us if we can forgive someone who sins against us, then God will forgive us for our sins. I knew I had forgiven her when I had to minister to her. I remember telling God that He had jokes. I had to minister and speak life into the woman who broke up my home. Forgiving them set me free to be able to love again. No bondage!

The last step in my recovery process was reading a book titled *What Becomes of the Brokenhearted* by Michelle McKinney Hammond. This book helped me to understand that God was concerned about my pain. Psalm 34:18 tells us that the Lord is close to the brokenhearted and saves those who are crushed in spirit.

As I navigated through this book my emotions were all over the place, but it helped me to get in order. Each chapter had questions I had to answer, so it made me dig deep and be honest with myself. I had to look at how this happened and what I did wrong in this marriage. God showed me my mistakes and He also showed me why I became that person.

As I continued my journey to healing, my prayer changed. First, I asked God to mend my marriage, but it changed to "God, let your will be done." I knew that God knew what was best for me. In the process of being put back together, I learned to trust Him. It was not about what I wanted; it was about what was best for me, and God knew it.

Jeremiah 29:11 – "For I know the plans I have for you, declares the Lord, plans to prosper you and not to harm you, plans to give you a hope and a future."

I leave you with this. When you are going through a hard situation, you have to lean on God. God is your help. This was the most difficult thing I had to deal with in my life; being broken by someone I trusted and loved and to seeing my children's world just ripped apart. All I can say is thank you, God, for caring about little old me.

I give thanks to all the people who were there during this difficult time. Minister B., thanks for the many phone calls where you let me vent but you spoke life into me. Koby, thanks for walking out of work with me and getting those tears to stop. GeGe, thanks for going to court with me. I appreciate you all so much, but God will reward you for taking care of His daughter.

Pivotal Shift

Dr. Twila Blossom Jones

Bio:

Dr. Twila Blossom Jones has a great deal of enthusiasm for helping people to become the best version of themselves. She has chosen her passion for health and wellness as a platform through which to impact the masses to live at levels of optimal health. She uses her expertise and training as a chiropractor, former NCAA Division I Track & Field athlete, and former math educator to accomplish this mission.

She attended the University of South Florida, where she obtained her Bachelor's Degree in Mass Communications, Agnes Scott

College (post-baccalaureate program), and Life University, where she earned her Doctorate of Chiropractic Degree.

Dr. Twila is a chiropractor who loves to get to the cause of the dysfunction and pain in the lives of her patients so that they can thrive in every aspect of their lives. She is married to Travis Jones. They live in Stone Mountain, GA with their three children, Twila Adrian, Taylor, and Travis, Jr.

Shifts and Life Lessons

There have been many pivotal points in my life that have caused me to shift into my higher self, God-ordained path, and purpose and into my unique destiny. I have been blessed to have had and created instances that were joyful, heartbreaking, devastating, inspiring, and miraculous.

Situations such as moves to new cities, the death of a father, being a top athlete, graduations, heartbreak, layoffs, career changes, marriage, becoming a mother, surviving marital infidelity, starting and running a business, sexual harassment, betrayals, and financial setbacks.

When I think of those situations, they rocked me to my core and altered my mindset on how to trust and love people. They gave me confidence in myself, bolstered my faith in God, revealed my true friends, and showed me who and what I was truly made of.

However, with all those lessons learned, there is NOTHING more heart-wrenching and pivotal than watching your mother suffer and dwindle away.

My Mother's Struggle

As I write this, my mother is sick. In fact, in all transparency, she has been sick for months. She has suffered with bronchitis, pneumonia, walking pneumonia, upper respiratory infections, and COVID-19 multiple times. Since 2023, she has taken rounds of antibiotics, steroids, and albuterol breathing treatments.

What started out as the seasonal flu or cold, that she would only get around the holiday season, turned into her getting sick four to five times a year.

As a health care provider, I was perplexed. My instinct as a woman and mother to nurture was heightened. I remember talking to my brother, who was a core man (equivalent to a Certified Nursing Assistant) in the Navy and we both agreed that she wasn't diagnosed properly—they missed something.

For years we would say this to her. Our mother wasn't too eager to listen to her children tell her how to live ANY aspect of her life, especially since she always reminds us that she is Mom. That's her way of politely telling us to back up and remember our place. BUT we just couldn't dismiss this unusual, strange constant wave of sickness.

The Turning Point

Early this spring, she began to share that she would be out of breath when she walked up the steps to her bedroom. She said she felt "winded." What took her a moment to catch her breath turned into minutes, and then 15 minutes. Then the 15 minutes turned into 20 minutes of intense coughing attacks after she would walk up the stairs or eat.

She lost a massive amount of weight—rapidly. Meals that were once a regular plate turned into portions that could fit on a dessert plate. She feared the coughing that followed eating. She ate enough to stay alive but not enough to live.

This summer, I asked her to come to Atlanta to get properly diagnosed. I begged her. I pleaded with her. It was out of selfish interest and pure fear. I needed to put and keep my eyes on her.

We are blessed to have a doctor in our family who is second in charge at a major hospital in Atlanta. She assisted us with getting the proper care. What we thought would be only a day visit turned into a week-long stay full of tests, blood draws, x-rays, ultrasounds, and CT scans.

She was properly diagnosed with pulmonary fibrosis and interstitial lung disease. Her other healthcare providers had missed this. My brother and I were correct.

The Reality

Her oxygen levels were below normal and she had developed pneumonia. She was treated with oxygen, antibiotics, and steroids. She did improve. Her spirits picked up and she seemed relieved and hopeful.

But when I researched the disease, my heart sank. It is considered irreversible and requires a constant supply of oxygen.

When she came to my house from the hospital, she was no longer the same. She couldn't breathe on her own and required oxygen. The compressor was delivered. The green oxygen tanks became a part of our home. The hum of the machine became a familiar sound. Seeing her with a tube in her nose became as normal as seeing her in her glasses.

But as we waited on appointments and insurance approvals, she began to dwindle. She became feeble in body and depressed in spirit.

The Daughter's Heart

The mere thought and saying it out loud is deeply horrifying because my shero is down. My personal superwoman can't fly her cape and come to my rescue.

The little girl in me is mortified. However, the grown woman—the mother, wife, community leader, and chiropractor—is holding it together by a thin thread of faith.

Long showers have become my wailing room. The long drive home has become my sanctuary. These are the places where I cry out to God with my most authentic, fragile emotions.

I am beyond angry that she is suffering. I know we all must leave this earth one day, but I imagined her leaving in her nineties, peacefully in her sleep. Not like this.

Lessons in the Pain

My children, my patients, my friends, my leadership programs—these have become what I call healthy distractions. They remind me of my purpose and fuel my soul when depression sets in.

I've learned that I can only control what I can control, even if it's just respecting the way my mother wants to handle her health.

At this point, I am uncertain how to be a daughter and how long I will get to be one. That title—daughter—was my first. And I don't want to lose it.

I stand on the faith my mother taught me. She showed me that God is the only one you can rely on. Still, I wonder: why must she struggle now? Why must my shero's breath be stolen?

We don't talk like we used to. She is too fatigued and I am too scared to face the reality of her mortality.

The Shift

This has caused me to shift. To pivot. To realize that life is short—so enjoy it. Forgive. Love hard. See the world. Jump at every opportunity that fuels your God-ordained purpose, soul, and destiny.

If you have a dream or burning desire, go for it. If a vision won't leave your thoughts, do it. My mother always said life is just a vapor and this life goes quick. She is right.

We must go to Martha's Vineyard—that is her dream. I pray she gets better, even just to see it for a day.

Swallowed But Not Forsaken

Elder Kenneth Bryant

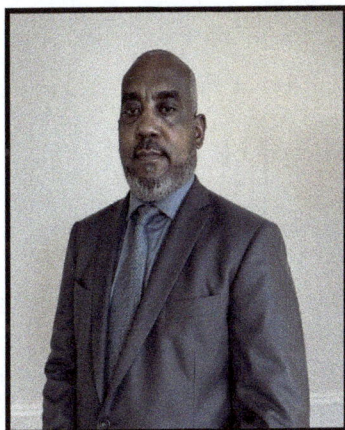

Kenneth Bryant was born in the hard streets of Brooklyn, where survival shaped his strength and faith. After serving 21 years in the NYC Department of Corrections—rising from Officer to Captain—he retired and moved to Georgia, where his spiritual journey deepened.

Joining a local church in 2018, Kenneth became an ordained minister in 2020 and was elevated to elder in 2022. His debut book reflects the hard-fought transformation from flesh to spirit and the grace that restored him. Not a perfect man but a devoted one, Kenneth continues to grow closer to God every day—living proof that transformation is possible through faith.

A Night Out

It had been a long time since I'd gone out, especially to a lounge. I decided to attend a coworker's birthday party and invited my childhood best friend Chris to join me. It was March 2022, as COVID was winding down.

During the pandemic, I had spent my time studying to become a minister, obedient to my Heavenly Father's call to go higher. I didn't fully understand that calling until later.

At the party, I had a couple of drinks and was feeling good—surrounded by people and especially my best friend. He was a business owner and a flashy, decadent type. He was buying drinks for everyone and showing off his money. I've never been a heavy drinker, always more of a social one. But that night, my flesh was in control and I was resisting God. I began to consider giving up my calling to chase the dreams my friend and I once had of being *high rollers in the entertainment industry*. In that moment, I wasn't just tempted—I was being conformed.

The Warning of Romans 12:2

Romans 12:2 — *"Do not conform to the pattern of this world, but be transformed by the renewing of your mind."*

Paul warns us not to let the world squeeze us into its mold. The "pattern" refers to the system that pulls us away from our purpose. That night, I was tempted to trade my calling for comfort. Every believer faces a moment when the world's whispers are louder than the Word. That moment at the party was mine.

So how do we stay focused on the Word, the truth, and the way?

1. **Meditate on Scripture**

Psalm 1:2 — *"But his delight is in the law of the Lord, and on his law he meditates day and night."* Reading the Bible is essential, but we must also internalize it.

Proverbs 4:23 — *"Above all else, guard your heart, for everything you do flows from it."* Be careful what you consume—music, media, movies, or conversations. Protect your spiritual sacred ground with your life.

2. **Seek Wisdom Through Prayer**

James 1:5 — *"If any of you lacks wisdom, let him ask God."* Prayer isn't just communication—it's calibration. Ask God to sharpen your discernment, expose distractions, and strengthen your focus.

The Arrest

The night ended and I was having one of the best times of my life. On the drive home, I was still amped up from the party. I had taken my eyes off the Lord and was deep in my comfort zone. I forgot about the speed reduction near my house—from 45 to 35 mph—and was pulled over for speeding. The thrill vanished instantly.

The officer asked me to take a breathalyzer. As a former law enforcement officer, I declined, knowing how inaccurate those tests can be. Refusing a sobriety test meant automatic arrest. Just like that, I was in the belly of the big fish. My life changed forever.

When it was time to make my one phone call, I couldn't remember my wife's number. I stayed calm in the holding pen and a childhood memory came to mind—Bruce Lee in *Enter the Dragon*, wrapping his nunchaku around his neck and sitting in stillness amidst chaos. That's exactly how I felt: no panic, no fear. I sat, breathed, and prayed. My stillness prepared me to face whatever was coming. I felt God's presence.

When the detention officer called my name, I thought I was being sent to a housing area. I mentally prepared to change into prison clothes. But the officer laughed and said, "Are you trying to stay? You've been bailed out."

My eyes lit up with joy. In the lobby, my wife was waiting. I asked how she knew I was in jail. She said when I didn't come home, she knew something was wrong. She prayed and began calling hospitals and jails until she found me. Then she contacted a bail bondsman and got me released.

Psalm 46:10 — *"Be still and know that I am God; I will be exalted among the nations, I will be exalted in the earth."*

The Book of Psalms teaches us that stillness isn't passive—it's a posture of trust where surrender becomes strength.

Belly of the Fish Moments

There are times when we find ourselves in the belly of the big fish. When that happens, we should:

1. **Pray**

   Jonah 2:1 — *"From inside the fish Jonah prayed to the Lord his God."*

2. **Acknowledge the Reality**

Jonah 2:5 — *"The engulfing waters threatened me, the deep surrounded me."*

3. **Recommit to God**

Jonah 2:9 — *"But I, with shouts of grateful praise, will sacrifice to you. What I have vowed I will make good. I will say, 'Salvation comes from the Lord.'"*

4. **Stay Still and Remain in Perfect Peace**

1 Kings 19:12 — *"After the earthquake came a fire, but the Lord was not in the fire. And after the fire came a gentle whisper."* Elijah didn't find God in the noise but in the stillness.

Redemption and Promotion

I was a free man again, but the consequences remained. I had to hire a lawyer, notify my job, and submit paperwork to the DMV within 30 days to avoid license suspension. It was one of the worst times in my life. My job suspended me immediately. I paid my lawyer over $6,000. It was a stressful time, but I stayed still and kept asking God why this was happening.

God gave me favor and allowed me to return to work after two weeks. There was so much overtime that I worked every day and quickly paid off my lawyer. My court case dragged on for six months. Then I received a letter from church promoting me from minister to elder. I knew it was a sign from God. I cried, knowing God had stepped in.

The next day, my lawyer called to say the arresting officer had agreed to reduce the charge. I knew it was the work of God.

Conclusion: My Belly Moment and Jonah's Redemption

Just like Jonah, I found myself in a place of isolation, consequence, and reflection. Jonah's belly was a fish—mine was a jail cell. But both were divine appointments, not punishments. In the belly, Jonah prayed, acknowledged his condition, recommitted to God, and waited in stillness. I did the same.

I also understood when God told me to go higher. He wanted me to develop a relationship with Him and get to know Him, and I complied.

Jonah's story didn't end in the fish and neither did mine. God used that moment to realign me with my purpose, to remind me of my calling, and to show me that grace still flows even in the depths.

If you've ever found yourself swallowed by circumstance, remember: the belly isn't the end—it's the beginning of transformation.

Let your belly moment become your breakthrough. *Salvation comes from the Lord.*

THE POWER OF THE PAUSE

Keiona Stewart

Bio:

Keiona Stewart is an entrepreneur and business owner with over 13 years of experience in the insurance industry. She understands what it means to walk through seasons of change with nothing but faith to hold on to. Navigating the challenges of building businesses has taught her that faith steadies you when outcomes are uncertain. She has seen firsthand how surrendering personal plans allows God to open the right opportunities in His timing. Her journey reflects both the vulnerability of waiting and the joy of answered prayers. Through her work and her personal life, Keiona encourages others to live boldly, with faith as the anchor for every decision. As a contributing author, she shares how leaning on God has shaped her path and sustained her through challenges—reminding readers that no step of faith is ever wasted.

The Power of the Pause

My shift didn't come from a dramatic tragedy in the past. It came in the present, through something that sounds so small but has completely changed my life: learning the power of the pause.

For me, pausing has meant learning not to push when I want to be right, learning not to force when I see the answer clearly, and learning to trust Jesus in the space where I'd normally try to control. That pause has become my shift—in my relationships, in my business, and most of all, in my faith.

When Silence Speaks Louder Than Being Right

For much of my life, I noticed a pattern: I often ended up being cast as the villain in someone else's story. It didn't start that way. I would step in with good intentions, trying to solve problems, untangle confusion, or bring clarity. But by the time it was over, my direct delivery and my need to prove the point left the other person defensive—and suddenly, I was no longer the helper. I was the antagonist.

I didn't like the person that made me appear to be. I didn't want to carry the weight of being remembered as someone who always had to win. That's when I realized my shift was going to look different. It wasn't about changing who I was at the core—assertive, logical, a problem-solver. It was about learning how to pause before my strengths turned into stumbling blocks.

Understanding My Own Wiring

Part of what made this shift possible was learning more about how my brain works. If I ask a question and don't get a direct answer, my mind doesn't just let it go—it locks on like a puzzle piece missing from the box. I loop around it until it feels solved.

For some people, that's no big deal. But for me, it could hijack conversations and push me to demand clarity long after others had moved on. At one point I started wondering, *Maybe this is ADHD or maybe it's a form of autism.* I haven't sought a diagnosis, but just exploring those possibilities gave me language for what I was experiencing.

It helped me see this not as a flaw but as something that needed managing with intention. That awareness itself was a gift from God. It gave me permission to pause and ask, *Is this really about them—or is my brain just stuck in a loop because it didn't get closure?* Sometimes the most faithful choice is to leave the question unanswered and let Jesus quiet my mind.

Walking Away Before Becoming the Villain

One of the biggest shifts I've made is learning to walk away before the conversation turns me into the villain. And by walking away, I don't always mean physically leaving. Sometimes it's choosing not to push, not to force my version of truth in that moment.

Proverbs 17:27–28 says, *"The one who has knowledge uses words with restraint, and whoever has understanding is even-tempered. Even fools are thought wise if they keep silent, and discerning if they hold their tongues."*

I used to think being right was the goal. Now I see that sometimes wisdom looks like restraint. It looks like holding space for someone else to reach their own conclusion.

Learning to Love Differently

Sometimes I think about love the way that song "If You Let Me" by Sinéad Harnett feels—not in the exact lyrics but in the spirit of it. Love isn't about being perfect; it's about showing up better the next time.

That resonates with me because my shift isn't about proving I'll never mess up again. It's about learning to love people in a new way—with more patience, more pause, more space for them to figure things out on their own.

For me, trusting Jesus looks like this: not trying to be the hero, not trying to be right, but asking, *"If you let me, can I love you better than I did before?"*

Trusting Jesus in the Pause

Everything in me still wants to win the argument, prove the point, or close the loop. My natural instinct is to push. But when I feel that pressure rising in my chest, I've started to invite Jesus into the pause.

I'll whisper a prayer: *"Lord, help me let this go. Help me value peace over being right."*

And something shifts. The burden lifts. The urgency to prove myself fades. I remember that Jesus is the one who makes things whole. My job is not to control—it's to love.

The Business Shift

This shift hasn't only shown up in relationships. It's been just as real in my business. There came a time when, in order for my business to grow and go to another level, I knew I could no longer interact with every team member in the same way. Not only was it time to shift the tone, it was time to shift the conversations.

Tone mattered because I've always been direct. That directness worked when I was hands-on in every detail. But for the business to grow, I had to take my hands out of the mix. Growth meant trusting others to carry what I once carried myself.

If I hadn't already learned how to pause and surrender, I couldn't have made that shift.

The First True Pause

Looking back, the original growth moment came about five years in. I had done all I could to keep things moving forward. I prayed and prayed, asking God what to do next, and the answer was always the same—though it took me a long time to hear it.

One day, it became clear: I was looking for actions I could take, trying to solve it all like a puzzle, when all He wanted was my belief.

It sounds simple, but that was my first true pause. I had to stop navigating and focus on my relationship with Him. Because the foundation of faith isn't strategy—it's belief.

My assignment in that season wasn't to list people to call or mentors to chase. It was to stop, to step back, and to trust. To relinquish control. And imagine that—an assertive, forward-thinking, A-type, direct communicator being asked not to do more but to pause and believe.

That was where my true shift began.

Closing

My story is one reflection among many in this book, but it's the one God gave me: the shift into the power of the pause.

I've learned that pausing doesn't mean weakness. It means strength. It means trusting Jesus to guide the conversation, to guide the business, to guide me.

And if He can meet me there—in the moments where I'd normally push, prove, and press harder—then He can meet anyone. Because sometimes the most powerful shift isn't about changing your circumstances. It's about learning to pause, trust, and let Him lead.

Didn't You Say, God What Now?

Dr. Tracey Starkes Gonzales

Bio:

Dr. Tracey Gonzales is an ordained teacher of the Gospel who holds a doctoral degree in biblical studies and a master's degree in business administration. She is a retired Army officer with 24 years of service and she is also a retired government civilian employee. She is the founder of Virtue of Women charged with equipping and empowering women. Dr. Gonzales' greatest joy is found in serving her family and community. She has served as the Director of Public Relations;

Regional Director for Education; Church Administrator and is currently serving as the Director for the GROW Ministry: Gaining Real Obedience in the Word Ministry. She is determined to live life and work to the glory of God because tomorrow is not promised.

It is a wonderful thing when you get to a place in your life where you feel like you can truly hear and discern the things of God. I have been walking with the Lord, I mean truly walking with Him, since 1998. But can I tell you that even with this being the case that I still have crises that challenge my entire belief system? I am walking through a season of transition right now. This transition is stretching me and taking me outside of myself so much so that the pressing is becoming oppressive. I know that everyone says that change is constant, which I do not want to hear right now. It is not the change that is challenging but the sudden silence, the lack of movement, the unfulfilled expectation.

I had for the last five or so years heard many say that I need to move back to Georgia. It is not that I was resistant to the idea, but I refused to move because of what people were praying and not what God was saying. I had learned the painful lesson of moving when God did not give the movement order. Those three years almost made me lose my mind, my money, and my mission. I was angry with God because He did not show up and fix the things I broke with my decision to move when and where He did not send me. I shifted from alignment with His will and purpose for my life.

So, I was not going through this again. I patiently waited for the whisper of God's voice. Every year I placed this possibility before Him hoping that the Holy Spirit would lead and guide me. He was completely silent on moving period, so I did not move. I was content living in my current home and state with my current job and income. But then one day He spoke. It was soon after the new year (2025) during my quiet time when I heard just the word "new" and I delved into the word and let it settle in my spirit. New (kainos) means made, to come into being, not before known, or recently discovered. I felt release and confirmation when Pastor Chris laid out the church's vision for 2025. It was to be a year of "New Beginnings" and a new faith level. I did not really understand what that would entail until I began to walk to and through my "New" season.

Shortly after I embraced the new, I found myself facing three questions that shook me and made me feel like I was unstable in my faith walk. But the real question was even more frightening for me to face. *Has it been me all this time?*

Didn't I Hear You Say Retire from My Good-Paying Government Job?

It had always been my desire to retire at fifty-five, but considering that I am now fifty-seven that did not happen. I was fine with this because I am a person who needs to keep moving. I also liked the freedom my income gave me in ministry and life. I was too comfortable with the extra. I am a retired Army officer, so I receive a nice retirement check every month along with disability. The sacrifices I made in time and body garnered a comfortable income, if managed right after retirement; however, after six months of not working I could not take it, so I took a government job that paid well for my expertise.

The beginning of this year brought clarity for me through prayer and fasting. I felt peace coming upon me that this was the year that I could finally retire from the government. I dropped my retirement package and felt good about it. As I began to make preparations to transition to the regimented schedule of everyday office work, I began to wonder what life would look like after my second retirement. As I stepped into full transition mode with complete excitement things began to happen in my life that required me to spend a good bit of money. I was looking at my bank account balance continuing to decrease. Now I was frustrated and fearful because I thought God said He was going to sell my house quickly, but five months later I had not even received an offer. See, I was depending on the equity that had built up in my home; it was supposed to be my nest egg and provide me with peace of mind. My lips were saying the right things every time someone asked about my retirement and house, but my heart, mind and peace were in shreds. I felt like I had been tricked by God because Proverbs 3:5–6 says, *"Trust in the Lord with all your heart and lean not on your own understanding; In all your ways acknowledge Him, and He shall direct my paths."* Isn't this what I did? Isn't this what I had been doing all these years? I did not just decide to quit my job. I laid my desire to retire before You and You spoke. Right?

Didn't I Hear You Say, "Move Back to Georgia?"

I have felt for a while that You would move me back to Georgia when it aligned with Your plan for my life. I have wanted to be closer to my family for such a long while. It has been hard living in Alabama in isolation from my family for almost ten years from my family. Illness after illness and hurt after hurt. I am not saying that during this time my family was not available, but it takes almost five hours from one side and almost three from the other side. Any emergency was a challenge that I tried to manage on my own too many times, some successfully while others were a complete mess. Yes, I have friends in the city and church family, but sometimes even that is not enough and I just wanted my family. So, when I received the release to sell my house and move to Georgia, overwhelmed and relieved, I took action. I began to make trips to the area I felt like You planned for me to move to in order to search for a home. Trip after trip nothing but constant disappointment. I was on my knees in tears wondering what I missed. I had an expectation that You would just show me and that it would be quick. You already told me to downsize, I am good with that, and to stay in my budget, and I am good with that as well. Am I being greedy with my requirements? Okay, I will compromise on some of those too. Come on now, Lord, You know that I have my standards. I am having this whole conversation with Him because He is my Father and we talk for real! I am calling to You. Please, Father, I cannot hear You anymore. Why are You silent now, Daddy? Do not leave me to my own devices; not now. You know that I am a planner and I will produce a plan when it looks like my timeline is misaligned. You know I cannot help it because I am a perfectionist and You made me this way.

Didn't I Hear You Say, "Connect with This Church?"

I have been supporting this church in Georgia for years and just knew without a doubt that when I did finally move this church would be my home church once You released me from Alabama. So, naturally, when I started looking for homes in the area, one of my requirements was that it was less than 20 minutes from the church. This church loves God and teaches His Word. These people are my family and we have been doing ministry together for a while. But now I find myself questioning if this is where You want me to serve during this season of my life. If I do not make this my home church, will they break ties with me? I did say that these people are my family, right? Lord, tell me what to do. I do not have peace when I think about joining anymore and every time I make a move without peace it is wrong. See, if the devil can disturb my peace, he can disrupt my entire world because love and peace are the foundation of all of God's Fruit of the Spirit. Without love and peace my joy, hope, kindness, goodness, faithfulness, gentleness, and self-control will soon fall. My walk was in danger and that was not acceptable for me. I could not go back to a life without God, but I felt myself struggling in my faith walk. I know better, but I began to look at my circumstances. My faith and expectations of God have always been a source of strength and encouragement for me in my relationship with Christ, but the enemy was turning my belief in God's might against me.

My job, my move and my church are all central to my total spiritual, physical, mental, and emotional well-being. So, the three-pronged attack has been remarkably effective during this season of my life. The enemy's subterfuge has been undermining and subverting my walk with God. I keep questioning myself, trying to wait for the Holy Spirit to show me the way. Where is my confidence? Was it me or You speaking?

Questions

The unresolved questions drove me to 21 days of prayer that aligned with my Church's annual 21 days of prayer. I did not realize that when I began this season of prayer it would expose cracks in my armor that I had not perceived. It is not a pleasant feeling to lay before God in stupidity and brokenness. It is, however, the best place to redefine, refocus and further shape my relationship with the Holy Trinity. I lay there before the throne naked and ashamed that I had allowed myself to sink into despair. Three questions formed in my mind and heart.

1. **Is Everything Alright with My Relationship with God?** Am I hearing from the Throne Room? We all face this question in our walk eventually. However, the perfect storm of faith for me presented challenges that seemed insurmountable. When I was honest with myself and God, I was not as confident in the decisions I had made saying that God was leading me. It is not hard to tell whether God is speaking to you when you are pursuing things against His Word, but when it is perfectly in alignment with His Word then you can find yourself on shaky ground like I was at that moment. In these times we must remove all distractions and sit in His presence with His Word and do not move until we know and hear His voice. If what you are planning is contrary to what He says in His presence immediately turn from this behavior or plan; you must follow and heed what He says. He spoke little pieces of the plan to me over the total 21

days; it was not instantaneous, but it was Him. He spoke through the Word and dreams.

I am glad that He spoke and I am sure that it was Him because my peace returned and His love covered me.

2. **Is Everything Alright with My Relationship with Other People?**

Church challenges are never easy; even when you are not directly involved, it is hard to witness. It can comprise the ministry or even break it apart if the foundation of the church contains immature Christians. Mature Christians should be able to walk through differences with the leading of the Holy Spirit. I also know that confusion in the church challenges me on every front. Strife in the church displaces my peace and I will avoid it if possible. No church is perfect and they all have some disorganization because of people. We just need to find the one that God has planted us in to thrive and contribute to the upbuilding of His Kingdom. I have served with a ministry in total confusion and stayed too long when God told me to leave two years before but I did not because of personal attachments. The break became messy and hurtful. If I had just left when He spoke, relationships would have survived the parting. When we fail to respond to God's plan there is a cost. So, this time I will not commit to what He has not ordained. I may produce fruit in the house but never what the divine plan has already predestined when we walk properly in His perfect will not His permissive will. I will continue to support but not join unless God says so later, but right now the answer is to be still.

1. **Is Everything Alright with My Relationship with Stuff?**
If you want to intensify the attack of the enemy, spend your time getting closer to God. When I decided to commit all the challenges of my life to God for the annual 21 days of prayer so that I could gain clarity and ensure that I was aligned with His Holy plan, the flood gates opened. First attack: Car accident in my new car and the needed part backordered.

Now I am out of pocket for the rental.

Second attack: Terrible pains in my body.

Third attack: Delay in loan approval for my new home. The challenges drove me to my face not to my knees. I found myself prostrate before the Lord. This was just where God needed me to be. It was here that He was able to get my mind off the things and this body that He gave me. If He gave me these things anyway what was my concern? Why had I allowed the enemy to whisper in my ear? Why had I wavered in my faith? Why? Comfortability had become my friend. I got into my routine in my walk with God. Attend service, serve at a service, watch service of ministry that I support, prayer every morning, MIT, Bible study, prayer on Saturday, and start over again. But it was just a small crack, right? What is small to us is insurmountable to overcome without the intervention of God once the enemy slips in. It was in my most intimate moments with

God that He delivered me, lifted my heart, and turned it fully back to Him.

Prayer, honesty, and actions are the answers He gave to realign me with His plan that will lead me into this season in the exact place, position, and posture that He designed especially for me. Thank You, Lord, for loving me so well. Even when I almost fainted You showed up! I am still waiting for something to resolve and align, but my eyes are focused on You.

BUT GOD

Dr. Shuante Bingham

Bio:

Dr. Shuante Bingham is an instructional designer, community leader, and lifelong advocate for growth and transformation. A devoted wife and mother of four, she embraces her calling as a virtuous woman who finds strength and balance in family and faith. With a passion for inclusive education and innovative learning, she designs accessible curricula that empower both learners and educators. Deeply rooted in her South Gwinnett community, Shuante serves in youth sports leadership, parent-teacher initiatives, and scholarship programs that inspire the next generation of scholars and athletes. She finds her greatest joy in family and draws strength and direction from her faith in God, which guides her commitment to service, creativity, and purpose.

Whether building opportunities on the field, in the classroom, or through community ventures, Shuante believes that true joy is found in growth, family, and faith-filled togetherness.

"Whew, child, it has BEEN A RIDE. Like a WHOLE ride. I admit that sometimes I sit amazed at the journey and results. Every once in a while, the corner of my mouth will turn up slightly as I mentally thank GOD for HIS mercy and congratulate myself for a job well done. But most days, I sit focused, overly anxious, cautious, wondering what my next step needs to be. GOD said not to have a spirit of fear, but some days I am paralyzed with it. Always afraid of not being accepted, not being good enough. Just know ... YOU ARE ... even though most days it won't feel that way. You have an absolute heart of gold. Things may not always come together as planned. No, you're definitely not as far financially or professionally as you should be, BUT one thing people will unanimously say about you is that when someone is in need or something needs to be done, you are the person they trust to accomplish the goal. And honestly, that is the best gift of words we could ever imagine. Your beautiful children always shake their heads while simultaneously grinning when they see you. Proud of the effort but confused by the motivation. If only they fully understood the journey. If only they fully understood the value of the words ... BUT GOD."

I still remember the day I wrote these words. It was 2018. A few nights before, I was sitting in my room, completely overwhelmed, exhausted, and frustrated. My head was swirling full of negative thoughts, questioning my existence and purpose. *Why am I here? Am I just in the way? What have I truly accomplished?* It felt like nothing was going right. You ever just have those moments where even though everything on the surface looks in order, underneath the veil is chaos and confusion?

I have a beautiful house, but everything in it seems to be rusting or breaking. I have a loving marriage, but communication and trust issues keep me from fully embracing the partnership. My kids are clean, fed, active in activities, and have a vibrant social life, but I feel like I don't have enough love or knowledge to help them fully reach their potential. I have a job, but there is no passion or genuine interest in what I am doing.

The 'buts" were tearing me down. Hopelessness and helplessness had started creeping into the forefront of my mind daily.

My eyes were swollen and deep red from the waves of sniffles to full sobbing. My brain was so cloudy and dark. I remember wanting to redirect my thoughts. I wanted desperately to speak joy and happiness into my life, but the feelings of emptiness and sorrow rang too loud in my ears. Despite having a loving, supportive husband and four incredibly gifted, kind-hearted children, I felt incredibly alone. Alone in a world where I believed no one could possibly understand me or genuinely want me around them. These words bellowed between my ears. It was so loud and clear, I started to wonder how it could not be true. And at some point, I decided, even if the words were not true, something was clearly wrong with me to think about life in this manner.

So I made the decision. A decision that admittedly occupies a portion of my mind to this day. A decision not absent of thought but absent of clarity. That night was meant to be my last night, or so I thought.

Here is where God's proclamation comes in, that what was meant for evil He turns for good. Here is where the word "but" takes on new power, no longer a weight but a breakthrough. And here is where I cry out with all passion and gratitude ... BUT GOD!

Disgusted with myself for how I was feeling, but also convinced it was necessary, I succumbed to my feelings of emptiness. The next part I promise to this day feels like one of those classic movie recalls when you have good and bad dialogue on your shoulders. The voice broke through my thoughts with a command that was not to be denied or dismissed.

Me: It's time. I'm tired.

Voice: But wait.

Me: Why? I can't. It's too much.

Voice: Nothing is too much. Lean on ME.

Me: I've tried everything. It's too much. Nothing helps.

Voice: You haven't tried everything. Lean on ME.

Me: I don't understand. I pray. I go to church. It doesn't help. I'm tired.

Voice: You don't trust ME. Lean on ME.

Me: I just need help. I'm lost. I don't understand.

Voice: Where is your faith? Have I ever left your side? Think back, child. Have I ever left your side? Lean on ME.

Y'all, I PROMISE those last words hit my spirit with a vengeance that shattered the box of negativity that had me trapped. It was like I was standing in a museum of mirrors, looking at my pain and anguish reflect back at me, but the mirrors began to shatter as I remembered the moments that followed those original painful thoughts. All those moments of embarrassment, hurt, failure that felt like they could not be resolved, BUT GOD. The memories of how the next moments, next morning, next opportunity always presented itself in a way that was undeniable, GOD loved me.

I continued to cry hysterically, but it was no longer from the sorrow I felt for myself; it was from gratitude that God chose to speak to me in the moments I needed Him most. Even in those moments, I remember pleading to God to just help me understand how to move forward with unwavering faith to help me not reach that dark space again. Now, I'd love to say that God spoke to me that night with all the keys of success, but that is just not true. What I did hear as an overwhelming, undeniable resolution was, "TRUST Me."

The storm in my mind cleared and I woke up the next morning with a new commitment to give myself to God in the best way I can. Hear me clearly. I am FAR from perfect. Let us all be mindful of the ever so true words of Pastor Donnie McClurkin: "We fall down, but we get up." This has been a continued journey. Fear and uncertainty still creep into my forethoughts at times. There are still occasional days of darkness. And, let's be real, there will always be pain.

But, as I continue to make this journey of breakthrough towards living in faithfulness and not in fear, my personal commitment to lean in on God's Word and promises has strengthened.

Here are some of God's Word and promises that get me through the harder days...

If God has done it for others, why wouldn't HE do it for me? Psalms 34:3–4 encourages us to lean into God's power and presence, thanking HIM for delivering us from our fears. God has promised us transformation, but that doesn't happen in shallow waters of faith. Isaiah 43:2 assures us that God will be with us through the hardest moments if we keep our faith and belief in HIM. Faith is released by the words of your mouth. Prayer, Praise, Worship, repeat. Consistency matters. Don't break the cycle. 2 Corinthians 4:13–18 reminds us that no matter how heavy our world feels, no matter how much the pain hurts, God has the final say. We do not know the path God has set for us, so we should just continue to put our trust and purpose in HIM. What God has for me is for me. Jeremiah 29:11 emphasizes that when you're in God's lane, there is never any traffic. Don't be preoccupied with the movement and success of others. His dominion over our lives is purposeful.

Stop showing the devil how to make you quit. Acknowledging God's authority and position over your life annoys the enemy and changes the atmosphere. Ephesians 6:11, 13 stresses the urgency and importance of leaning into God's armor of protection (scripture, prayer and faith) to resist the devil's tactics to distract and discourage us from God's purpose over our lives.

Above all else remember GOD is LOVE and to give yourself GRACE. He is your source of comfort. He is the light needed when all else feels dark. God is the wisdom when understanding is missing or lost. He is the peace when all you can feel is chaos.

The "buts" that once wore me down, filling me with doubt and heaviness, are now the very places where God's power has shown up in my life. What once sounded like defeat has become the turning point of my story. Every time I have thoughts like, *But I can't ... but I'm not strong enough ... but I don't see the way forward,* I consciously seek to remember God answered with His own declaration: "But I can. But My strength is made perfect in your weakness. But I am the way." The word that once symbolized my limits has now become the evidence of His limitless power.

As I stand in gratitude, I'm reminded of a beautiful phrase boldly preached by my husband: "Don't ask why this is happening to me; learn to ask why this is happening for me." What once felt like a burden has now become a blessing. What once looked like an obstacle has become the very tool God used to shape me, strengthen me, and draw me closer to Him. So I close with this testimony: every trial, every tear, every 'but' in my story has been transformed by His hand.

And when I ask, "Why is this happening for me?" I see His purpose, His power, and His love at work today. When I look back, I no longer see the weight of doubt but the breakthrough of grace. And with full passion and gratitude, I can only proclaim ... BUT GOD!

The Seasons of Me

THE SHIFT THAT SAVED MY LIFE

Elder Clarence D. Johnson

Bio:

I am an ordained minister and teacher committed to nurturing spiritual growth and academic excellence. With years of experience leading worship and classrooms, I create inclusive spaces where individuals deepen their faith and expand their knowledge. I blend thoughtful instruction with compassionate mentorship to empower others, foster meaningful relationships, and inspire lifelong learning and service.

The Shift

An experience that significantly transforms one's life could be advantageous, often leading to a shift in perspective or a profound reorganization of one's life and priorities. By Elder C Johnson

This publication is dedicated to assisting you in self-healing and uncovering your personal, spiritual and ethical journey. It does not aim to impose any ideology or set of values but rather to reveal the most admirable aspects of your character.

Greetings, I am Elder Clarence Johnson. Let us now examine the evolution of my life and observe how it underwent a significant transformation (A Shift) that has influenced every facet of my existence. It's a personal journey of self-healing that initiated a change that will continue indefinitely.

My early years were marked by a blend of joy and tension. As I was raised in a household predominantly composed of women, I learned how they think and respond to controversy. It developed a heart of passion for others. I never had the opportunity to meet my father due to him being married with a family. My mother once presented me with a photograph of him, but due to its dark quality, I was unable to discern his facial features. I never had the chance to confront him. However, there were other men in my life who filled the void left by his absence, instilling in me a Christ-like character.

I have always had a strong interest in musical instruments. I was proficient in playing the trumpet during my middle school years and I even ranked among the top three trumpet players in the concert band. This was my means of escape from the turmoil that surrounded me. My family, however, was quite deceitful and manipulative. They were constantly engaged in disputes and arguments over trivial matters. Their behavior was characterized by greed and a desire for what others had.

Upon completing my high school education, I enlisted in the navy, where I acquired discipline and character. However, in my personal life, I encountered challenges in maintaining a relationship. I entered into relationships with sincerity and transparency, only to be exploited for my possessions and loyalty. Concurrently, my relationship with God was minimal during this period. I was preoccupied with self-centered thoughts and concerns about others' perceptions of me.

After my service in the military, I came home, got a job and found myself back in the same situation. My family were still deceiving and greedy. It was no better at my job. There was a position open for management. There were several people highly qualified for the position included myself, but they wanted us to train a younger person with a college degree and with no experience to be our manager. Well, that didn't settle well with me. I became angry and vindictive. I found myself in trouble with the law facing with a sentence totaling 200 years. When asked by the arresting officer why I committed the crime, I responded that I was fed up of people manipulating me and others for their personal gain. While awaiting trial the severity of the sentence set in. Not having a relationship with God and no idea how to communicate with Him, let alone how to pray, I began to speak out loud the entire Book of Psalms every day at least three times a day.

My mother was extremely concerned about me, so she engaged a root worker to assist. I was given specific tasks to undertake in order to mitigate this situation. Upon leaving my mother's residence on my way to court, I made a conscious decision to relinquish control to God. As I entered the court building, the arresting officer approached me and informed me that I needed to inform the judge of my intention to withdraw for lack of representation, which was approved.

I continued to read from Psalms and the new trial date was set. Prior to entering the courtroom, the same officer approached me and reiterated the same information. I responded that I believed it would not be effective this time, but he persisted. I conveyed the same sentiment to the judge, who declined, but the district attorney suggested he required a reset and it was approved.

Prior to my next court appearance, I received a call from the court. The voice on the line inquired about my identity and then identified me as Clarence. The caller expressed that there was a significant amount of love for me, given the circumstances I was facing. They requested that I meet with them one day per week for the next thirteen weeks and the charges would be dismissed.

I successfully completed the thirteen-week program and the charges were dismissed. However, it was challenging to secure employment due to my arrest record, which indicated the reason for my arrest. Employers were reluctant to hire me as they believed I had served time for this offense. I was advised that if I received a letter from the courts stating I did not serve time for this arrest, they would consider hiring me.

I visited the district attorney's office to obtain this letter. The secretary informed me that I seemed very familiar. I responded that I was unfamiliar with either the secretary or her daughter. She then inquired about the reason for this charge being expunged from my record. She proceeded to explain the process of expungement. Three months later, I received another letter from the court confirming that the charges had been expunged. This marked the point of my transition with GOD.

I may not fully comprehend God's methods, but I am certain that it is the sole path to remain in His presence.

It is written in Isaiah 55:6–9 KJV:

[6] Seek ye the LORD while he may be found, call ye upon him while he is near: [7] let the wicked forsake his way, and the unrighteous man his thoughts: and let him return unto the LORD, and he will have mercy upon him; and to our God, for he will abundantly pardon. [8] For my thoughts are not your thoughts, neither are your ways my ways, saith the LORD. [9] For as the heavens are higher than the earth, so are my ways higher than your ways, and my thoughts than your thoughts.

Your journey will not be straightforward. You are being directed by divine intervention, despite your past shortcomings. Remember, God was aware of you before you were conceived.

Also bear in mind that, in this life, you will encounter challenges and difficulties. Hardship is an inherent aspect of human existence. These experiences can be perceived as tests of faith, opportunities for personal development and purification.

This is not the moment to be apprehensive; it is a pragmatic alert that pursuing a spiritual journey does not ensure a trouble-free existence. However, it also serves as an inspiration that these challenges do not catch God off guard and that success is always attainable through Him.

Challenges can be perceived as prospects for individual advancement, education, and enhancing resilience. The fundamental idea is that, despite adversity, there is optimism as Jesus has already secured ultimate triumph through his death and resurrection.

I understand your query, "Where should I commence?" You should commence with your heart, wholeheartedly dedicated to learning as per the teachings of God. Trusting Him even when there's no comprehension.

This encompasses the process of renewing your mind. It entails consciously capturing negative thoughts, reflecting on God's Word, seeking guidance through prayer, and consistently substituting detrimental beliefs with uplifting ones to foster personal development and righteousness.

2 Timothy 3:16–17 tells us

[16] The whole Bible was given to us by inspiration from God and is useful to teach us what is true and to make us realize what is wrong in our lives; it straightens us out and helps us do what is right. [17] It is God's way of making us well prepared at every point, fully equipped to do good to everyone.

Study, meditate on, and saturate your mind with Scripture to fill it with truth and replace harmful thoughts.

Kindly consider questioning the legitimacy of restrictive beliefs and kindly substitute them with inspiring, Christ-centered viewpoints.

There will inevitably come a point in one's life when they may find themselves fatigued and disheartened by their current lifestyle.

Thus, you have experienced a change. This underscores the transformation from external compliance to internal dispositions, leading you to relinquish your previous methods to God's will.

It is written in John 15:5 NIV:

[5] "I am the vine; you are the branches. If you remain in me and I in you, you will bear much fruit; apart from me you can do nothing."

This analogy illustrates the principle that believers must have a close, abiding connection with Jesus to produce spiritual "fruit". Just as a branch cannot bear fruit on its own and must remain attached to the vine for life and nourishment, believers must remain in Christ to be spiritually fruitful and to truly be his disciples.

If this is you, make a conscious decision to start your shift by accepting JESUS as your Lord and Savior. Say this prayer with me.

Lord Jesus, I believe You are the Son of God, that You died for my sins and rose again. I ask that You come into my heart, forgive my sins, and make me a new person. I accept You as my Savior and Lord and surrender my life to You. In Jesus' name, Amen."

Congratulations, your shift has begun. I encourage you to seek a Bible-based church. Attend a Bible study group to enhance your relationship with Christ. Become active in your community service, leading others to their shift.

I love you and am so proud of you.

Now unto him who is able to keep you from stumbling and to present you before his glorious presence without fault and with great joy to the only God our Savior be glory, majesty, power and authority, through Jesus Christ our Lord, before all ages, now and forevermore! Amen.

POWER OF GRACE

Marion " Pete" Cunningham

Bio:

My name is Marion "Pete" Cunningham. I was born in Sarasota, Florida. Life has tested me in ways I never imagined. Through faith, resilience, and determination, I have learned to rise above adversity and turn pain into purpose. My journey has taught me the value of hope, compassion, and perseverance.

Dedications:

To my beloved mother, Bettie Jean Carter, and brother, Rashad Anton Cunningham. Their spirit remains woven into every step of my journey. My story is dedicated to their memory, a reminder that love never fades and even in their absence, they continue to inspire, guide, and dwell in my heart.

Acknowledgment:

To my husband, Gregory, whose steadfast love and encouragement have made this work possible.

The weight of my past became too heavy to carry alone. I thought I could manage it. I tried to keep moving forward pretending the pain did not exist. But the truth was the longer I carried it the heavier it became. Instead of surrendering to defeat, I made a choice to cling to God's promises. His Word reminded me that He gives beauty for ashes, strength for weakness, and hope for the hopeless. I had to release people and things from my life that were once cherished. They no longer aligned with where God was leading me. This journey was not just about change but also surrender. I realized transformation does not occur until we let go and let God.

As I reflect, I see how God's love, grace, and mercy carried me when I did not have the strength. It is only because of God I can tell my story. My prayer is that my journey will benefit others who are trapped in the challenges of the past. There is hope, healing, liberty, and redemption in the love of God.

Christmas was the one time our family felt together. My mom made it magical with bright lights in every window, velvet reindeer in the glass, and a beautiful tree filled the room with warmth. Her cooking, cheer, and the brief belief in Santa made me feel free and joyful. After my youngest brother was born, everything changed. My parents fell into drug addiction and separated. My mother tried to care for us, but her struggle overwhelmed her. That is when my childhood ended and I had to grow up.

As a child, I became the caretaker of my brothers. With my father gone and my mother often absent, I learned to survive alone, masking fear with strength to keep us together. At home, I made meals from whatever we had and helped my brothers with their homework. When the food ran out, we went to bed hungry, relying on school meals and occasional soup kitchens to get by. I washed clothes by hand, hanging them on the fence to dry and ironing them if they were damp. When the electricity was disconnected, I lit candles. I did not want my brothers to worry. Eventually, we had to live with our grandmother. This was not an escape from the realities of my life but was another form of survival. My grandmother was a strict disciplinarian; it was like going from one hell to the next. Our nutrition and developmental needs were barely met. She was verbally and physically abusive. Her constant criticisms left deep emotional scars. Today, I often struggle when looking at myself without hearing her voice.

When social services finally stepped in, we were placed in foster care. The system wanted to separate us, but I refused to let that happen. I begged and pleaded with the judge, terrified that if they separated us, I might never see my brothers again. To my relief, they agreed to keep us together. We became wards of the state and were sent to the Florida Baptist Children's Home. It was not easy, but we were together, bound by blood and survival. The day we left for the children's home was emotional and frightening. We had never been away from our family. When we arrived, we received a warm welcome, but the adjustment was hard. We were the only African American kids there, and at first, we felt out of place. In time, the awkwardness faded. The move was a blessing in disguise.

Finally, we could be kids and experience a normal life, surrounded by kind people who remain part of my life today.

My mother was serving a prison sentence for drug-related charges with plans to complete rehabilitation before regaining custody. She proved to the court that she could care for us. When custody was granted, I suggested she bring us home one at a time. My youngest brother went first, then the middle one, and I stayed at the children's home a little longer to give her time to adjust. At the end of my sophomore year of high school, I moved back home. I was so excited to be reunited with my family. For a moment, my life felt complete.

However, after a few weeks of being home, my mother relapsed. What should have been a joyous reunion quickly became my worst nightmare. I gave up a stable life at the children's home. I was thrust into a life I was not prepared for. My anger turned to hopelessness and then into depression. Even though my relatives knew of our struggles, they did not offer support. Once again, I was responsible for my brothers.

We hid our struggles, living off my father and his disability checks. It barely covered expenses, so I made desperate payment arrangements with the landlord and utility companies.

Often, I would rush home from school to make sure I got the support checks before my mother did. Eventually bills piled up, utilities were shut off, and we were evicted. I had no time to think, only to react. I packed what I could, sold what I could, and reluctantly reached out to social services. My youngest brother was placed back in foster care. I was heartbroken, but I knew this was the best option. My middle brother went to stay with a friend and I was left alone.

My family refused to take me in; a kind neighbor welcomed me despite having three kids, one with a disability. I focused on graduating from high school, worked full-time, and eventually moved in with a classmate. It was not ideal, but it worked. I stayed close to my brothers throughout.

I was angry at my parents for their selfishness. Then, on my birthday, my mother showed up, tired and tearful. She thanked me for caring for my brothers, apologized, and told me she loved me. I felt something shift as I heard the Holy Spirit whisper, "Forgive her." She hugged me and gave me a tan jacket, a sign I still mattered. It was the last birthday we celebrated together.

After graduation, I attended the University of South Florida. I started the process of gaining legal custody of my youngest brother. Unfortunately, because of my age and low income, I lost the custody battle. The judge told me to try again in a few years. Though devasted, my brother reassured me that he would be okay.

One Halloween, while trick-or-treating with my brother, he suggested we check on our mother. I agreed at first, but something deep inside told me not to. I just knew we should not go. After our night of fun, I took him back to the foster home. Not long after I got home, I received a devastating phone call. I was told my mother had been killed in a drug-related car incident. I was too emotional to drive, so a close friend drove me home. When we arrived, the street was blocked with yellow caution tape and swarming with police. My friend's car had not even come to a complete stop before I jumped out. I ran as fast as I could toward the scene. I saw my family and then my mother. I began running towards her, desperate to reach her, until I was restrained. She lay in the street uncovered, lifeless, and alone. This image of my mother will be in my mind forever.

I was financially responsible for my mother's burial. My father had promised to help but disappeared when it mattered the most. The death of my mother broke something inside me. I lapsed into depression. The image of her lying in the street replayed repeatedly in my thoughts. I struggled to remember what she truly looked like prior to her death. I was afraid to sleep. My dreams frequently would take me to that dark street, forcing me to relive the moment. The pain consumed me; it took a toll on my body. I had difficulty eating and lost weight as a result. I knew I could not continue this journey on my own. I needed help. In my brokenness, I turned to prayer and asked God to heal me from the despair.

Through prayer and faith, I felt God working in my heart. The nightmares slowly vanished. The haunting memories of my mother did not fade, but by God's grace, I began to see her smile, hear her voice, and feel her love.

My brothers and I were close, but I had a special bond with my youngest brother. We were not just siblings; we were friends. We spent much time together, laughing, talking, and sharing life. He was full of energy, joy, and his smile lit up the room. I taught him how to drive and did my best to guide him through life's challenges. Despite the obstacles he faced, he pushed forward with determination. When he graduated from high school and went to college, my heart swelled with pride.

Five years had passed since my mother's death and I was still navigating the pain of her absence. My youngest brother was attacked and stabbed at a nightclub. He was rushed to the hospital, and at that moment, my world shattered again. Gathering what little strength I had, I rushed to his side. When I walked into the hospital room, I saw him lying there, fighting for his life. I held his hand, whispered to him that I loved him, and I felt him squeeze my hand. That moment is forever etched in my mind. Moments later, he was gone. I had lost my mother and now my brother. They meant so much to me. It felt as though tragedy had become a companion, shadowing every step of my journey.

In darkness, I knew I had to hold on. I had to carry their love and memory within me. Losing my brother broke me, but it also shaped me. It deepened my compassion, strengthened my faith, and ignited a fire to keep moving forward, not just for myself, but for them.

I was stricken with grief for years and was unable to celebrate the holidays. Then I remembered how much Christmas meant to my mother and how special she always made it. To keep her memory alive, I created a memorial Christmas tree in her honor. Every year, I decorate the tree with birds in honor of both my mother and brother. What was once a season of sorrow has become a season of remembrance, love, and hope.

Neglect and tragedy led me to surrender to God. I could not carry life's weight alone, but His grace gave me new vision and understanding. Letting go of relationships that no longer aligned with His purpose was painful but necessary. My past shaped me; God molded me.

Breaking Free from Legalism

Phyllis Brumfield

Bio:

Phyllis Brumfield is a devoted mother, mother-in-love, and grandmother. In her fifties, she said "yes" to God and embraced her assignment of simplicity. She now encourages others to develop a relationship with God and be open to the unique assignment He has gifted them with.

2 Corinthians 5:20 — We are therefore Christ's ambassadors, as though God were making his appeal through us. We implore you on Christ's behalf: Be reconciled to God.

I was born and raised in New Orleans, Louisiana, in a family deeply rooted in the Southern Baptist tradition. My parents and grandparents were God-fearing people who wanted me to know the Lord and live according to His Word. Religion was woven into the fabric of our family life, yet for me, it always felt confusing, overwhelming, and sometimes restrictive. I saw others around me believe so deeply, while I quietly wrestled with questions I didn't dare speak out loud.

As a child, I often tried to bargain with God. "Lord, if You do this for me, I'll be faithful. If You give me what I want, I'll change." I treated faith as a transaction rather than a relationship. When He didn't respond the way I expected, I shrugged it off and continued on my own path. That pattern followed me well into adulthood.

From my twenties through my forties, my religious life was mostly ritual. I attended church on Sundays, tithed ten percent, listened to sermons, felt momentarily inspired, and left it all behind the sanctuary doors. Prayer happened only when I wanted something and I relied on others to interpret scripture for me. I treated God like a genie, believing that my obedience earned my blessings. I really thought if I tithed and performed some activities, I was heaven bound.

Between the ages of twenty-five and thirty-five, I explored other religions—Catholicism, Islam, Buddhism—searching for meaning. Each offered beautiful rituals and traditions, but none satisfied me. It was not the religion, it was me. Church had become social; I attended to see new fashions, hear gossip, or feel part of a community. I had lost sight of God entirely. My mindset was simple: give God my ten percent, ask for what I want, and expect Him to deliver. I wasn't interested in a relationship with God; I was not sure what I wanted.

Even when I noticed subtle signs—warm touches, lingering thoughts, gentle nudges—I intentionally ignored them. I thought if God wanted to communicate, it should be dramatic: thunder, lightning, unmistakable commands. I liked who I was and didn't want to change. My faith was shallow, but I did works for the church and I was content to live in my own version of a Godly life, my way.

The Shift

Everything began to shift during a work assignment in Dallas, Texas. I was determined to continue my religious ritual—find a church, attend, give an offering, and send my tithes home.

After visiting several churches that didn't resonate, I happened to hear Pastor Tony Evans on the radio. His calm, steady voice immediately stood out from other preachers. He wasn't hollering, demanding attention, or focusing on fear. Instead, he told stories, applied scripture to everyday life, and made faith feel approachable. I was drawn in and knew I had to experience his ministry in person.

The following Sunday, I found myself at Oak Cliff Bible Fellowship, sitting quietly among the congregation. Pastor Evans preached about legalism, a concept I had never heard of and certainly did not understand. He explained that legalism is the belief that salvation or righteousness can be earned through works or strict adherence to rules rather than faith in Jesus Christ. It focuses on outward behavior, man-made rules, and self-righteousness, often creating fear, oppression, and judgment.

As I listened, I felt a weight lift from my shoulders. This was the SHIFT. I was in Dallas for a four-week work assignment, sitting in a church I had never heard of, listening to a pastor I knew nothing about. Well, the assignment lasted six months and the learning experience was a life-shifting experience.

For years, I had believed that enjoying life—singing, dancing, or expressing joy—was sinful. Pastor Evans explained that God cares about the state of our hearts, not outward perfection. I realized that my lifelong fear of judgment had been misplaced; God had never condemned me for enjoying His creation or celebrating life. That sermon was revolutionary for me. It changed my entire perspective. I am aging myself, but I purchased the cassette and played it repeatedly, letting the message sink deep into my mind and heart. This encouraged me to read the Bible with intention.

Through Pastor Evans' teaching, I began to see God's love in a new light. I didn't need others to dictate what He wanted from me; He would reveal it directly. I began to read, study, and pray—not demanding, "God, give me this," but asking, "God, what would You have me do? How can I be a better person?" I started to notice God's "language" in my life: gentle nudges, lingering thoughts, the warmth of a breeze. I was learning to recognize Him, not just perform rituals. I desired a relationship.

I also came to understand that God knows exactly how to communicate with each person. I remembered Thomas in John 20:25, who said he wouldn't believe unless he saw the marks of Jesus' crucifixion. I was like Thomas—a believer who needed tangible proof. God knew this about me and communicated with me by touch in a way I could perceive, gently nudging me toward faith without overwhelming me. He knows each of us and meets us in the way we can receive Him.

Transformation

Transformation began gradually. It was not anything magical that happened overnight, weeks, or months, but unmistakably it happened. I acted on the nudges God placed in my mind, choosing joy and integrity over fear and routine. I began to close out the noise of other people's opinions and expectations, focusing on developing my personal relationship with God. I noticed the difference between God's gentle guidance and the chaos of people's influence. Where Satan might tempt or deceive, God offered direction, comfort, and love in ways I could recognize.

As I followed God's guidance, my life began to change. I found myself making decisions with clarity and confidence. Old habits that no longer served me faded away. I was no longer walking in fear, constantly anticipating the next blow. I laughed more freely, worshiped with abandon, and embraced creativity and self-expression—knowing now that these were gifts from God, not sins to fear.

For Late Bloomers

For late bloomers—those who feel it's too late to begin—I want to assure you: God meets you exactly where you are. Your age, past mistakes, or years of neglect do not limit Him. He knows your unique "God language" and will reach you in the way you can understand and receive. Some will hear God's voice in prayer, others in thoughts, touch, scripture, or even music. Be patient, stay open, and trust that He will make Himself known in a personal, undeniable way.

If everyone developed a relationship with God in their pre-teens, teens, or even in their twenties and thirties, they wouldn't be able to truly witness to others that it's never too late to come to God—because they wouldn't have had that experience.

Two Crystal-Clear Truths

1. **God walks with you even through fire.** Life will bring trials, temptations, and moments of fear. Satan may try to tempt or deceive you, but God's presence will sustain you. I have walked through fire with God by my side, feeling His guidance even when the path was hot and uncertain. I have faced challenges that could have overwhelmed me, but I felt His strength holding me up, His gentle nudges steering me safely through. Unlike Satan, who will push you into danger and leave you there, God walks with you, step by step, and never abandons you. I would walk a mile on hot coals with God before I would step a block with Satan on a cloud. God's love and guidance are real, tangible, and dependable—He will meet you in your moment of need, in the way only you can understand.

2. **You must clear distractions to hear God.** To experience God's presence fully, you must intentionally remove noise— the opinions of others, societal expectations, or misguided

advice. I had to move people out of my way to find my path with God. When I intentionally closed out the distractions, I could recognize His voice, feel His guidance, and act on the nudges He placed in my mind. This allowed me to develop a personal, unique relationship with Him. God knows each of us intimately and communicates in ways tailored to us. He will use your "God language" to guide, comfort, and teach you—if you make the space to listen.

Today

Today, I walk with God intentionally. I respond to His nudges, act on insights, and embrace the mission He has entrusted to me. I have experienced a transformation that is real, lasting, and deeply personal. My story is proof that no matter your age or past missteps, God can transform your life if you are willing to listen and follow His guidance.

Late bloomers, take heed: your season has not passed. God's grace is sufficient, His timing perfect, and His love unwavering. He knows your heart, understands your experiences, and will meet you in the way that only you can receive.

Leave people and their legalism behind. Follow God and He will allow you to realize the gifts that He has bestowed on you. Remember—the gift of one's presence is a wonderful gift.

FINDING GOD'S PURPOSE IN LIFE SHIFTS

Terrelle Shepard

Bio:

Terrelle Shepard, MBA, CFP, is a seasoned financial professional with a certification in Financial Planning. She holds many licenses in the financial industry. Terrelle is a Marine Corps veteran with a passion for helping individuals and businesses thrive. As the founder of Total Choice Financial Solutions Group, she brings over a decade of experience to the finance sector.

Terrelle is dedicated to empowering communities through education, smart financial planning, and business development. Her passion is driving by God and seeing others win.

Life, Love, and Loss

Life, Love, and Loss; these three L's shift a person in ways unimaginable. Each season of life brings its own terrain: the joy of blossoming beginnings, the ache of unexpected endings, and the stillness found in between. But through it all, I've learned God doesn't waste a single shift. Every change, every heartbreak, every breakthrough was a divine setup for something greater, something more purposeful. This is my journey through the seasons of me, where pain met purpose and loss gave way to light.

I grew up close to my family and I've always known structure. Joining the Marine Corps shaped a part of me that desired order, discipline, and a drive to lead with confidence, even when I was uncertain. I took pride in getting things done, showing up strong, keeping everything in place, and no matter what, the mission must go on.

When I became a mother, that same mindset followed me into my home. I became a woman who wore many hats: mother, leader, provider, fixer, and, for a while, I thought I was managing it well. Life was full, sometimes overwhelming, but still in my control. At least, that's what I believed. But here's what I've learned: Life doesn't ask permission to shift.

It doesn't send a warning email. It doesn't ease you in. Sometimes, the seasons of life change in an instant and all you can do is hold on and hope your faith is strong enough to carry you through it.

My first major shift came in 2016. The kind of shift that shakes your identity, tests your faith, and makes you question everything you thought you knew about who you are and what God is doing in your life. It was the beginning of a breaking but also the beginning of a becoming. I didn't know it then, but that year would mark the start of a new season, not just in my life but in me.

This season of shift started with a loss. I lost my second-oldest sister unexpectedly, unknowingly, and without warning. One moment we were laughing and talking on the phone and the next she was gone. No amount of structure, discipline, or strength could have prepared me for that. Nothing in my training could teach me how to breathe through that kind of grief. I didn't just lose her; I lost a part of myself.

In that moment, I realized how fragile life really is and how quickly the people we love can be pulled from our grasp. That loss shook me to my core. It opened a door to a season I didn't ask for but one that would reveal just how much I needed God, more than ever before.

I experienced sadness, hurt, and anger; emotions that crashed over me like waves I couldn't control. I had so many questions and no answers that made sense. *Why? Why now? Why this way?* It felt unfair: it was unfair. I was searching for understanding, but what I found instead was revelation.

In that season, I came face-to-face with a truth that I, and many others, overlook. No amount of money, no level of success, no social status or material gain can protect you from life's ultimate reality; if you don't have your health, it means nothing.

My sister didn't get to grow old. She didn't get to see her life's full story. And in losing her, I realized how fragile we really are. How quickly it can all be taken. That kind of pain changes you; it changed me. It shifted my perspective on life and that was the beginning of me learning how to let go of things that didn't matter and start holding on to the things that did.

Life and love took on a new meaning. Losing someone close, so unexpectedly, shattered my illusions of time and permanence. I never imagined I'd lose my sister so soon. I thought we would have more laughs, more talks, more time to plan together. But when that was taken from me, I could no longer pretend that life would wait.

This loss woke something up in me. I no longer wanted to live life based on the image I thought would be pleasing to others. I was tired of performing, Tired of being who I thought I should be rather than who I truly was. And the saddest part of this shift, I didn't know how I got there.

During this time, I was married to someone who didn't love me but mostly couldn't love me, at least in the way I needed and deserved. But I was in it because I was raised to believe that marriage was the proper way, the respectable path. The "right thing" to do. But what good is doing the right thing when it's breaking you quietly?

That season taught me something sacred: Peace is holy too. I wouldn't keep going through the motions (amongst other things), not for appearances, not for tradition, not even for the sake of being a "good woman". I had to choose myself. I had to choose my truth. I had to allow God to rewrite my story or put it back on His path. I needed my children to see the real me. The me on a path of healing and wholeness, a version of me who didn't settle for survival but a version who fought for joy. This shift had begun, but it wouldn't stop there.

The breaking that became the becoming:

Soon after that shift, I found myself in another relationship. I mean, I jumped right back into what felt familiar, but this time, the familiarity came with deeper wounds. The lies were bolder. The control was heavier. The manipulation was stronger. And the cheating? Constant. But one night changed everything. After hanging out with associates, Mr. Familiar and I got into an argument that escalated into something violent. I let my anger take over; years of pent-up rage, betrayal, and brokenness poured out in a single moment. I almost took that man's life. Had it not been for one of my closest friends stepping in, begging me to stop, and pulling me out of that moment, you wouldn't be reading this chapter from me today.

In that moment, I wasn't thinking about my kids. I wasn't thinking about my life, my family, or my future. I was just releasing pain. But when it was all over, I realized I had come dangerously close to losing everything I'd worked so hard to build.

Something must change. For real this time! This was early 2018 and I made a decision: I was going to love myself like no one else ever had. I was going to rebuild from the inside out. Because I almost let someone with nothing to lose make me lose everything that mattered, especially my children. And I knew no one on Earth would raise them, protect them, and pour into them the way I would. I had shifted!

I got serious about my life, my education, my healing, my health, and my faith. I needed to get closer to God, to seek His approval, and I needed to learn to wait on God, not rush to fill voids with things or people that could never truly heal me.

I finished my bachelor's in science and earned my certification in financial planning. I received promotions at work. I was focusing on becoming the woman God designed me to be and the mother my children needed to see. Life was moving forward, but another shift was coming.

Life was moving forward. I was healing, growing, and staying focused on my purpose. But healing doesn't mean life stops shifting.

Around 2021, maybe early 2022, I found myself in another season I didn't see coming. My father's health had begun to decline and it took a toll on our entire family. For many weekends, I traveled back and forth to my hometown in Alabama, doing what I could to help, to comfort, to be present. I watched the strong man I had always known begin to fade, little by little. And still I tried to keep it together and push forward.

During this same time, my oldest son was preparing to graduate from high school and enlist in the United States Army. As I am with all my boys, I was proud beyond words, but also carrying the weight of the world on my back—parenting, school, work, and my father's illness—weighed heavily on me.

Then came the September morning that would shake us all. My youngest brother had been arrested, charged with a serious crime. I can remember the moment I got the call. I couldn't breathe. I jumped in my car and burned up the highway again, trying to understand what had happened, trying to help my family hold it together. We were navigating the legal system by day, home with my dad by night. Watching my father fight for his life while watching my brother's life change forever.

But the pain hit differently when I heard my father say, "He's tarnished our family name." That broke me.

In mid-2023, my father passed. This was a loss I still don't know how to put into words. I went back home to Georgia with a broken heart. I knew he was at peace, but I also believe he left this world with a broken heart of his own. Another shift had come. Another deep wound opened.

Still, I kept going. Smiling through the pain, carrying the weight of being strong for my mother, my siblings, and my children. But I was unraveling inside.

Then came March of 2024, when my youngest brother was sentenced to seven years in federal prison. A first-time offender. Seven years. It felt like time froze again. Our world was rocked once more. The grief, the anger, the helplessness, it came rushing in all over again. And through all of this, I was planning a wedding.

Amid all the chaos, I found my first love, my true love. I had found love again. It was someone I had known since I was fifteen, a connection that had lain dormant for years. We rekindled in 2020, long-distance at first, as we both focused on personal growth and our goals. This lover felt familiar yet safe, but challenging in a way that forced me to confront myself.

During this time, I was still navigating family crises, betrayals from friends and family, and the emotional rollercoaster of grief and anger. I often felt alone, unheard, and like no one truly understood the storms I was weathering. I carried all of that into my relationship, protecting my heart while trying to protect the little bit of myself I had left.

Yet, despite the pain, hope persisted. I got married in August 2024. It was our celebration of love, commitment, and a vision of a future that I had fought so hard to believe in. Life seemed to be moving forward finally.

But grief has a way of finding you when you least expect it. In December 2024, the unthinkable happened. My other brother, my friend, my confidant, my BFF, passed suddenly. We had spoken on the phone just the night before. I had no idea it would be the last conversation we would ever have. I felt it all over again: the shock, the despair, the questioning of why life seemed to keep taking from me. I was broken. I was afraid to feel happiness, to trust joy, because grief had taught me how fleeting it all could be.

The sadness, the anger, the nightly cries, they weighed me down. But God—always God. God sent me a patient partner. Someone who could withstand the whirlwind of emotions, someone who could hold space for the trauma and the healing simultaneously.

This was another season of shifting, not just in life but in me. I'm leaning on God like never before. I sought professional therapy to untangle the grief, the anger, the depression, and the fears that had piled up over the years. I'm learning to communicate better, to honor my health, my life, my worth, and my time. I became more accountable to myself, working daily to be a better partner, mother, daughter, and sister.

Through it all, as my shifts turned into seasons, I've learned one undeniable truth: God's purpose for my life is always greater than my plans, deeper than my pain, and perfectly aligned with His timing.

I no longer chase clarity. I trust God's calling.

Chapter Acknowledgements

First and foremost, I give all honor and glory to God—my source, my strength, and my guide. This chapter reflects His Grace and Mercy through every season of my life.

To my Husband, Sons, Family, and Close Friends, you give me strength. Thank you for your prayers, support, and encouragement. Your unwavering belief in me has carried me through every season of my life.

Next! Thank you, Amber K Abney. You presented an opportunity, but this was a journey of healing, growing, and emotional cleansing. To my co-authors, I appreciate all of you as we embarked on a journey together that allowed many of us to discover a new vulnerability and learn to live in our own truth, all while keeping God first.

To the readers, thank you for taking the time to read my story. May my journey remind you that purpose evolves, strength is birthed in silence, and God's plan is always greater than your own.

When God Says Shift

Elder Amber K. Abney

Elder Amber K. Abney, MBA is a woman of God, entrepreneur, and visionary dedicated to empowering women through faith, mentorship, and prayer. With over 20 years in the insurance and financial services industry, she blends business expertise with a heart for ministry. Amber is the founder of *Women Empowered By Prayer Ministries, Inc.* and visionary of *The Shift* anthology. She strives to live in the spirit of excellence while committing to helping women embrace transformation, build legacy, and walk boldly in their God-given purpose.

Acknowledgements

First, **I GIVE HONOR TO GOD,** who keeps me rooted in my daily walk. He guides my steps in all I do. Without His presence, wisdom, and love, this work would not be possible.

To God I give all the GLORY!

To My Parents: The Late Deacon Abraham Michael Logan & Sharon Williams Logan

May the life I live always reflect the harvest of your prayers, the strength of your hard work, the depth of your sacrifice, and above all, the beauty of your selfless love.

To My Daughter: Miss Chase-Symone

You are the greatest blessing of my life and the best part of me. Your presence has taught me the true meaning of love.

To My Grand-Pup: My Mazzi Man

Only God knew your presence would shift our entire family. You are a reminder of joy, comfort, quiet strength, loyalty, unconditional love, and the simple gift of being present.

To The Shift Collaboration Family

Your commitment and belief in this vision have carried me through the process of bringing "The Shift" to life. A simple conversation (with my life coach, Dr. David Wright) turned into a complete collaboration with seventeen beautiful souls. Each of you has left an indelible mark on this journey and I am deeply grateful for the way you showed up, contributed, and stood in alignment with the purpose of this work. Thank you for taking this healing journey with me.

Contact Amber K. Abney

Website: Iamamberkabney.com

Email: wempoweredbyprayer@gmail.com

Facebook: Women Empowered By Prayer Ministries Inc.

THE ALABASTER JAR

Before God could use me, He had to prune me, break me, and shake some things off me. There were seasons in my life when I didn't understand why I was being tested, why doors were closing, or why I was walking through fire after fire. But looking back, I can see that every moment of breaking had purpose. God was stripping away what I thought I wanted so He could give me what I truly needed. He knew I would need His anointing, His direction, and His power to carry the mantle on my life.

The alabaster jar has become a picture of my life. Just as the jar had to be broken to release its costly oil, I too had to be broken so that what God placed inside of me could flow out. The breaking hurt and the pruning was painful. The shaking left me feeling like my world was crumbling. But during it all, God was preparing me.

Like the woman who poured her oil on Jesus in love and surrender, I've learned that true worship means giving Him everything (even the parts of me I wanted to hold on to). Through my brokenness, God released the fragrance of His grace, His mercy, and His purpose in my life. What I once saw as a loss, I now see it as the very process that equipped me to do His work.

TODAY, I speak boldly where I was once silent. I have learned to trust Him where I once leaned on my own strength and understanding. While in the process of discovering The Real Amber K. Williams Abney (the Authentic, Joyful and FREE Woman), He showed me who I was when I shifted to Him. I am blessed to share three major events in my life, which caused me to SHIFT to Him.

Behind the Smile

You Are God's Child. Everything You Touch is Blessed. Blessed is the fruit of your womb! ALL THINGS WORK TOGETHER! YOU ARE WORTHY! YOU ARE MORE THAN ENOUGH!

Psalm 17:8

Keep me as the apple of your eye; Hide me in the shadow of your wings.

2 Timothy 1:7

"For God has not given us a spirit of fear, but of power and of love and of a sound mind."

Philippians 4:13

"I can do all things through Christ who strengthens me."

These are just a few words of affirmation and scriptures I had posted throughout my home. I had no idea the importance of having God's Word in the forefront of my mind every day, but I knew it was all I had to lean on.

At that time, my dearest brother Pete had traveled from Tampa, Florida to visit Chase and I at our home in Stone Mountain, Georgia. Almost immediately upon entering, he noticed the scriptures and affirmations posted on the walls, mirrors, cabinets, and even the doors. He asked about them with a genuine concern, wondering if everything was alright. I reassured him with a smile, letting him know that what he was seeing was not a sign of distress but of transformation. I was intentionally growing in my walk with Christ and aligning every area of my life with God's Word.

The truth was I was drowning in shame, embarrassment, guilt, and loneliness. Externally, I was a bubbly young wife and excited about being a new mother. However, internally, I was broken, and I carried the secret of being six weeks pregnant again alone. I was too ashamed to mumble the words out loud, and I was uncertain if I even had a marriage because of his absence.

I made sure to keep my wedding ring on in the public eye, not out of pride but out of fear of being questioned, fear of judgment, fear of exposing the reality I was trying so hard to hide. I had convinced myself that I was protecting my family, but honestly, I was barely surviving.

I was holding on to a marriage that didn't love me while secretly working three jobs to maintain the image. Internally, I struggled with my spouse who had befriended a family member who violated me as a child, and he was fully aware of it. Alone, I carried the pain because I didn't have the support of my family when I finally was brave enough to share it. I had so many questions, not realizing what I thought was love didn't exist. I carried the weight of my childhood into my marriage, because I never received the proper resources or tools to help me confront and heal from my past. Unbeknownst to me, I had inherited the behavior of watching the women in my family wear masks of strength while silently carrying pain. It had become my new 'normal' behavior.

My dear cousin saw through my smile and recognized the pain I was carrying. She sent me a New International Version Women's Study Bible, blank journals, and cassettes filled with words of encouragement. She told me she recognized that look in my eyes because it was one, she had known herself. With her prayers and love, I realized I could not hide behind the mask any longer.

In desperation, I began to seek God with all that I had left. I cried out for clarity, direction, and strength. I knew I could not allow my infant daughter to grow up under the shadow of my brokenness.

Not long after, a co-worker invited me to a "Friends and Family Day" service at her church. That Sunday, the bishop preached a message from John 15:5 that would shift the course of my life:

"I am the vine; you are the branches. If you remain in me and I in you, you will bear much fruit; apart from me you can do nothing." (John 15:5, NIV)

That verse pierced my heart. It revealed to me that Jesus is the true source of life and nourishment and that apart from Him, I could do nothing. I knew I had to stay connected to God to overcome where I was at in my life, so I embraced the essence of John 15:5. My life began to shift for His glory, and I faithfully served in that ministry for over 20 years.

The price of the oil on my life required surrender. It required me to walk fully in the presence of my Father and to yield to His pruning process. It required me to shift.

Boss Lady

Beaming with joy and excitement, I was finally walking into what I had prayed and sought God for over 13 years. I was opening my very own insurance agency, and I was officially becoming my own "Boss Lady."

What I did not foresee was the heaviness it would bring with balancing my personal and professional worlds. I was active in the local community, which was a blessing, yet it was overwhelming to combine. I desperately needed someone I could trust and support me as I navigated with the new responsibilities of being the "Boss Lady." I hired a vibrant young lady who was full of great ideas, who had an extensive career within the organization, but most important to me was that she looked like me! I trusted her and I placed the success of the agency in her hands. We were growing, hiring new staff, receiving recognition, and you could not tell me NOTHING! God was showing out, and my life was shifted forever.

Shortly afterwards, it all came tumbling down. I learned her behavior (behind the scenes) did not align with the company's contractual agreement and I was released in love (fired). I was told, "You did nothing wrong, but you just hired the wrong person to support you with the agency." A two-million-dollar agency built off commitment, sweat, tears, long hours, neglect of my family, etc. was shut down with a four-minute and thirteen-second conversation (4:13). As time progressed, I realized the company was fully aware of the young lady's actions and more than ten agencies were affected. I was embarrassed because the rumor was that we were stealing from the company, which was not true. I felt like a failure and my ego was bruised to the core. As I reflect, I believe it was their strategic way to restructure the organization under the guise of a scandal, BUT God had a different plan.

My dear sister friend reminded me that it was important for my daughter to see me overcome the scandal and I could not give up on her. In addition, I found comfort in speaking with my mother, who explained to me the responsibility had to fall somewhere, and it will always fall on you when your name is on the door. At the time, my church was in a series called GO BIG or GO HOME. My bishop reminded me that if God allowed me to build a two million agency, then what do you think He has for you on the other side!

Those conversations shifted me straight to my knees. It shifted me to the one who I knew could sustain me, to the one who shielded Shadrach, Meshach and Abednego from a burning furnace without a stitch of smoke on them, and to the one who knew me before I was even conceived in my mother's womb. I had nothing left to lose. I really needed God to intervene, and in that moment, He reminded me of John 15:5.

I began to understand that this wasn't really about the company or agency at all; it was about what God was doing in me. He stripped me down to the bare bones of who I was. My ego, my pride, even that "Boss Lady" title had to be laid down. The plan God had for me required a servant's heart. It was an elevation for God's Kingdom, which required the fullness of a willing vessel.

The insurance agency was never just a business, but it was a ministry. God's ministry. Yet, "I" had been treating it as though "I" was in control, and as if "I" was God Himself. "I" had started making decisions without Him. My ego had taken over, and "I" was not accustomed to the instant financial increase over my life. So, when the contract was terminated, it wasn't just the loss of work, it was a divine interruption.

Professionally, I was reminded that God must always lead. He had entrusted me with a little and I had no idea that greater was waiting on the other side of this ordeal. The journey He was calling me to required complete submission to Him.

I shifted.

What I once thought was a devastating two-million-dollar loss God transformed into a 10-million blessing on the other side. After laying down my pride and ego, I was able to witness the hands of God realigning my heart to His calling.

The Shift in My Soul

Dear Daddy,

I honor and celebrate the 43 precious years I had the privilege of calling you, my daddy. Although your transition shook me to my core, it also ignited something within me. It compelled me to go BOLDER for the Kingdom, to make my "YES" to God even LOUDER. Even in the pain of losing you, I could feel Him calling me higher and reminding me that my obedience would honor both Him and you.

You showed me that a man surrendered to God can be renewed, restored, and used in extraordinary ways. I had the privilege of witnessing your own "Saul to Paul" transformation (right before my eyes) and you made it your mission that your children would know God for themselves.

I have so many fond memories of you! I recall you taking me to Disney World when I was 10 years old. You made magic come alive and I still have my Mickey Mouse ears (35 years later). I remember being heavily recruited for track and field and I was uncertain of the best choice. I sought you for wisdom, but you lovingly reminded me that the decision had to be between God and me. The lesson to seek God's direction above all else still orders my steps today. Your heart was selfless, giving, and overflowing with love. I miss our early morning conversations about life, business, love, relationships, and, above all, God. Those weren't just simple conversations; they were a father pouring wisdom into his baby girl while preparing her heart for the journey ahead at the same time.

From an early age, you told me I was different and that God had chosen and set me apart. You encouraged me to embrace it, even when I was afraid of the judgment that might come. You spoke life into me and validated me as a young woman. My heart rejoices knowing that you lived to see the first fruits of the ministry journey you always believed was in me.

Our last moments in the hospital together have been anchored into my soul. I read the Bible to you, recited the Lord's Prayer, and I reminded you of the amazing father you had been to me. It was my way of giving back a portion of what you had poured into my entire life. Although you could not speak, I knew you heard my heart.

Every time God calls me to stand before a congregation, and each time I am entrusted with a platform to speak, I will carry your name with honor. I will tell the world who Deacon Abraham Michael Logan was to me.

Your transition shifted me into the arms of the only One who could breathe hope back into my spirit, restore my soul and give me the strength to move forward. For that, Daddy, I say thank you.

Thank you for preparing my heart for the world and for seeing not only who I was but also who I was becoming. I am proud to be your daughter, and I will carry your name, your legacy, and your faith within me forever.

With Love,

Your Baby Girl, Your Evangelist, Your Attorney, and Your Accountant
Amber

In closing, God showed me everything I endured was a part of His plan. There had to be someone to walk through the fires, so that God could receive the glory. It came with the cost of His glory being revealed in and through my life. To reach what was waiting on the other side, the alabaster jar had to be broken to sacrifice true worship, preparation, and submission in all areas of my life. And through that breaking, the fragrance of His glory was released.

I was the alabaster jar. I was cracked, heavy, and full of what I tried to hide. But when I poured it all out before God, He turned my pain into purpose. Today, I can BODLY share that every tear, every trial, every test was worth it because God alone receives ALL the GLORY! I can stand, smile, laugh, and carry joy in my heart because of the truth found in John 15:5: "I am the vine; you are the branches. If you remain in me and I in you, you will bear much fruit; apart from me you can do nothing."

HE SHIFTED ME...